THE HANDWRITING ON THE WALL

SECRETS from the PROPHECIES OF DANIEL

Volume 2

Dr. David Jeremiah

P.O. Box 3838
San Diego, CA 92163

Unless otherwise indicated, Scripture verses quoted are taken from the NEW KING JAMES VERSION.

Printed in the United States of America.

Contents

About Dr. David Jeremiah and Turning Point 4

How to Use This Study Guide 5

Introduction 11

13. Daniel in the Lions' Den
Daniel 6:14-28...................................... 13

14. God's Animal Parade
Daniel 7:1-8.. 25

15. Ancient of Days
Daniel 7:9-14....................................... 37

16. The Antichrist
Daniel 7:15-28...................................... 49

17. The Reign of Terror
Daniel 7:15-28...................................... 63

18. The Church and the Tribulation
Selected Scriptures 75

19. The Olivet Discourse Discussion
Selected Scriptures 89

20. Superpowers in Conflict
Daniel 8:1-8, 15-21................................. 101

21. Antiochus and the Antichrist
Daniel 8:9-14, 22-27................................ 115

22. God's Word and Prayer
Daniel 9:1-4.. 129

Resources... 142

Stay Connected.. 144

About Dr. David Jeremiah and Turning Point

Dr. David Jeremiah is the founder of Turning Point, a ministry committed to providing Christians with sound Bible teaching relevant to today's changing times through radio and television broadcasts, audio series, books, and live events. Dr. Jeremiah's common-sense teaching on topics such as family, prayer, worship, angels, and biblical prophecy forms the foundation of Turning Point.

David and his wife, Donna, reside in El Cajon, California, where he serves as the senior pastor of Shadow Mountain Community Church. David and Donna have four children and twelve grandchildren.

In 1982, Dr. Jeremiah brought the same solid teaching to San Diego television that he shares weekly with his congregation. Shortly thereafter, Turning Point expanded its ministry to radio. Dr. Jeremiah's inspiring messages can now be heard worldwide on radio, television, and the Internet.

Because Dr. Jeremiah desires to know his listening audience, he travels nationwide holding ministry events that touch the hearts and lives of many people. According to Dr. Jeremiah, "At some point in time, everyone reaches a turning point; and for every person, that moment is unique, an experience to hold onto forever. There's so much changing in today's world that sometimes it's difficult to choose the right path. Turning Point offers people an understanding of God's Word as well as the opportunity to make a difference in their lives."

Dr. Jeremiah has authored numerous books, including ***Escape the Coming Night*** (Revelation), ***The Handwriting on the Wall*** (Daniel), ***Overcoming Loneliness, Prayer—the Great Adventure, God in You*** (Holy Spirit), ***When Your World Falls Apart, Slaying the Giants in Your Life, 31 Days to Happiness—Searching for Heaven on Earth, Captured by Grace, Signs of Life, What in the World Is Going On?, The Coming Economic Armageddon, I Never Thought I'd See the Day!, God Loves You: He Always Has—He Always Will, Revealing the Mysteries of Heaven, Agents of the Apocalypse,*** and ***The God You May Not Know.***

How to Use This Study Guide

The purpose of this Turning Point study guide is to reinforce Dr. David Jeremiah's dynamic, in-depth teaching and to aid the reader in applying biblical truth to his or her daily life. This study guide is designed to be used in conjunction with Dr. Jeremiah's *The Handwriting on the Wall, Volume 2* audio series, but it may also be used by itself for personal or group study.

Structure of the Lessons

Each lesson is based on one of the messages in the *The Handwriting on the Wall, Volume 2* compact disc series and focuses on specific passages in the Bible. Each lesson is composed of the following elements:

- *Outline*

The outline at the beginning of the lesson gives a clear, concise picture of the topic being studied and provides a helpful framework for readers as they listen to Dr. Jeremiah's teaching.

- *Overview*

The overview summarizes Dr. Jeremiah's teaching on the passage being studied in the lesson. Readers should refer to the Scripture passages in their own Bibles as they study the overview. Unless otherwise indicated, Scripture verses quoted are taken from the New King James Version.

- *Personal and Group Application Questions*

This section contains a variety of questions designed to help readers dig deeper into the lesson and the Scriptures, and to apply the lesson to their daily lives. For Bible study groups or Sunday school classes, these questions will provide a springboard for group discussion and interaction.

- *Did You Know?*

This section presents a fascinating fact, historical note, or insight that adds a point of interest to the preceding lesson.

Personal Study

Thank you for selecting *The Handwriting on the Wall, Volume 2* for your current study. The lessons in this study guide were created to help you gain fresh insights into God's Word and develop new perspectives on topics you may have previously studied. Each lesson is designed to challenge your thinking, and help you grow in your knowledge of Christ. During your study, it is our prayer that you will discover how biblical truth affects every aspect of your life and that your relationship with Christ will be strengthened.

When you commit to completing this study guide, try to set apart a time, daily or weekly, to read through the lessons without distraction. Have your Bible nearby when you read the study guide, so you're ready to look up verses if you need to. If you want to use a notebook to write down your thoughts, be sure to have that handy as well. Take your time to think through and answer the questions. If you plan on reading the study guide with a small group, be sure to read ahead and be prepared to take part in the weekly discussions.

Leader's Guide

Thank you for your commitment to lead a group through *The Handwriting on the Wall, Volume 2*. Being a leader has its own rewards. You may discover that your walk with the Lord deepens through this experience. Throughout the study guide, your group will explore new topics and review study questions that encourage thought-provoking group discussion.

The lessons in this study guide are suitable for Sunday school classes, small-group studies, elective Bible studies, or home Bible study groups. Each lesson is structured to provoke thought and help you grow in your knowledge and understanding of God. There are multiple components in this section that can help you structure your lessons and discussion time, so make sure you read and consider each one.

Before You Begin

Before you begin each meeting, make sure you and your group are well-versed with the content of the chapter. Every person should have his or her own study guide so they can follow along and write in the study guide if need be. When possible, the study guide should be used with the corresponding compact disc series. You may wish to assign the study guide lesson as homework prior to the meeting of the group and then use the meeting time to listen to the CD and discuss the lesson.

To ensure that everyone has a chance to participate in the discussion, the ideal size for a group is around eight to ten people. If there are more than ten people, try to break up the bigger group into smaller subgroups. Make sure the members are committed to participating each week, as this will help create stability and help you better prepare the structure of the meeting.

At the beginning of the study each week, start the session with a question to challenge group members to think about the issues you will be discussing. The members can answer briefly, but the goal is to have an idea in their mind as you go over the lesson. This allows the group members to become engaged and ready to interact with the group.

After reviewing the lesson, try to initiate a free-flowing discussion. Invite group members to bring questions and insights they may have discovered to the next meeting, especially if they were unsure of the meaning of some parts of the lesson. Be prepared to discuss how biblical truth applies to the world we live in today.

Weekly Preparation

As the group leader, here are a few things you can do to prepare for each meeting:

- Choose whether or not you will play the CD message during your small group session.

  If you decide to play the CD message from Dr. Jeremiah as part of the meeting, you will need to adjust the group time accordingly.

- Make sure you are thoroughly familiar with the material in the lesson.

  Make sure you understand the content of the lesson so you know how to structure group time and you are prepared to lead group discussion.

- Decide, ahead of time, which questions you plan to discuss.

  Depending on how much time you have each week, you may not be able to reflect on every question. Select specific questions which you feel will evoke the best discussion.

- Take prayer requests.

  At the end of your discussion, take prayer requests from your group members and pray for each other.

Structuring the Discussion Time

If you need help in organizing your time when planning your group Bible study, here are two schedules, for sixty minutes and ninety minutes, which can give you a structure for the lesson:

Option 1 **(Listen to Audio CD)**	**60 Minutes**	**90 Minutes**
Welcome: Members arrive and get settled.	N/A	5 minutes
Getting Started Question: Prepares the group for interacting with one another.	Welcome and Getting Started 5 minutes	15 minutes
Message: Listen to the audio CD.	40 minutes	40 minutes
Discussion: Discuss group study questions.	10 minutes	25 minutes
Prayer and Application: Final application for the week and prayer before dismissal.	5 minutes	5 minutes

Option 2 **(No Audio CD)**	**60 Minutes**	**90 Minutes**
Welcome: Members arrive and get settled.	5 minutes	10 minutes
Getting Started Question: Prepares the group for interacting with one another.	10 minutes	10 minutes
Message: Review the lesson.	15 minutes	25 minutes
Discussion: Discuss group study questions.	25 minutes	35 minutes
Prayer and Application: Final application for the week and prayer before dismissal.	5 minutes	10 minutes

As the group leader, it is up to you to keep track of the time and keep things moving along according to your schedule. If your group is having a good discussion, don't feel the need to stop and move on to the next question. Remember, the purpose is to pull together ideas, and share unique insights on the lesson. Make time each week to discuss how to apply these truths to living for Christ today.

The purpose of discussion is for everyone to participate, but don't be concerned if certain group members are more quiet—they may be internally reflecting on the questions and need time to process their ideas before they can share them.

Group Dynamics

Leading a group study can be a rewarding experience for you and your group members—but that doesn't mean there won't be challenges. Certain members may feel uncomfortable discussing topics that they consider very personal, and might be afraid of being called on. Some members might have disagreements on specific issues. To help prevent these scenarios, consider the following ground rules:

- If someone has a question that may seem off topic, suggest that it is discussed at another time, or ask the group if they are okay with addressing that topic.
- If someone asks a question you don't know the answer to, confess that you don't know and move on. If you feel comfortable, invite other group members to give their opinions, or share their comments based on personal experience.
- If you feel like a couple of people are talking much more than others, direct questions to people who may not have shared yet. You could even ask the more dominating members to help draw out the quiet ones.
- When there is a disagreement, encourage the group members to process the matter in love. Invite members from opposing sides to evaluate their opinions and consider the ideas of the other members. Lead the group through Scripture that addresses the topic, and look for common ground.

When issues arise, remind your group to think of Scripture: "Love one another" (John 13:34), "If it is possible, as much as depends on you, live peaceably with all men" (Romans 12:18), and "Be quick to listen, slow to speak and slow to become angry" (James 1:19, NIV).

For Continuing Study

For a complete listing of Dr. Jeremiah's materials for personal and group study call 1-800-947-1993, go online to www.DavidJeremiah.org, or write to Turning Point, P.O. Box 3838, San Diego, CA 92163.

Dr. Jeremiah's *Turning Point* program is currently heard or viewed around the world on radio, television, and the Internet in English. *Momento Decisivo,* the Spanish translation of Dr. Jeremiah's messages, can be heard on radio in every Spanish speaking country in the world. The television broadcast is also broadcast by satellite throughout the Middle East with Arabic subtitles.

Contact Turning Point for radio and television program times and stations in your area, or visit our website at www.DavidJeremiah.org/stationlocator.

The Handwriting on the Wall

Volume 2

INTRODUCTION

In volume 2 of this three-volume study guide, we enter into the heart of Daniel's astounding prophecies of the future. And we note Daniel's reaction on two occasions—how the spectacular visions he received impacted him personally: "As for me, Daniel, my thoughts greatly troubled me, and my countenance changed; but I kept the matter in my heart" (Daniel 7:28). Again, "And I, Daniel, fainted and was sick for days; afterward I arose and went about the king's business. I was astonished by the vision, but no one understood it" (8:27).

Reading those words apart from their context in the book of Daniel makes one wonder what might have caused such a reaction in the prophet. But as soon as we read the description of the visions Daniel had, we're surprised he lived to tell about them at all!

Daniel's visions produced a far stronger reaction in him than the first experience we cover in this volume: his visit to a lions' den. He faced this test with the confident calm we have come to expect of this elderly saint. Told to give up his prayerful worship of the God of his fathers, or face death, he remained resolute in his convictions. He went to the lions' den confident that God's will was the best thing for him. And God obviously was not finished with Daniel since he was delivered safely from harm.

Next we get a glimpse of the visions that gave Daniel such a measure of discomfort. The visions of beasts were scary enough; but when Daniel received the interpretation, he realized that he was seeing the future of the ancient world laid out before him. And it was a future rife with upheaval. The Babylonians would be conquered by the Medes and Persians, but their rule over the Middle East would be replaced by the greatest conqueror the world had yet seen: Alexander the Great of Greece. The Hellenistic Empire would govern the world from Italy to the borders of China and as far south as Egypt for hundreds of years. It is said that Alexander sat down and cried at the height of his rule because there were no more worlds to conquer!

But Alexander's supremacy would come to a close in dramatic fashion at the hands (at the claws) of the fourth beast in Daniel's vision: Rome. This beast was "dreadful and terrible, exceedingly strong. It had huge iron teeth; it was devouring, breaking in pieces, and trampling the residue with its feet" (Daniel 7:7). We start to understand Daniel's physical, spiritual, and emotional reaction to these visions. It's one thing to read those words on the pages of the Bible, but it's altogether another to see them played out on the screen of one's mind in living color. Daniel was witnessing the greatest nations in history taking each other down, one after another.

But that's not all he saw. He saw God on His throne in heaven, and One "like the Son of Man" (verse 13) coming to establish His kingdom to rule over all the kingdoms of this world. And he saw one who would someday oppose the Son of Man, bringing terror and evil to earth's population. We see Daniel, in spite of all he witnessed in his visions, finding solace in the Word of God, falling on his face in worship of the God of Israel who had sent the Jewish people to Babylon and promised to return them to their homeland.

Daniel continues to prove himself to be the faithful servant of God we found him to be in volume 1 of this series—a man to whom God entrusted a picture of future events.

DANIEL IN THE LIONS' DEN

Daniel 6:14-28

In this lesson we see how God rescued Daniel from certain death in Babylon.

OUTLINE

The story of Daniel in the lions' den is so well known that "lions' den" has become a cultural cliché—and deservedly so since everyone faces difficult situations in life. Daniel's story yields principles and procedures for surviving life's hardest moments.

I. Daniel Preferred by Darius

II. Daniel Persecuted by His Enemies

III. Daniel Persistent in His Testimony

IV. Daniel Protected by His God

- A. The Displeasure of the King
- B. The Deliverance of Daniel to the Lions' Den
- C. The Distress of the King
- D. The Deliverance of Daniel in the Lions' Den

V. Daniel Proved by His God

VI. Daniel and Practical Applications

- A. The Probability of the Lions' Den
- B. The Promise of the Lions' Den
- C. The Purpose of the Lions' Den
- D. The Prosperity of Daniel

IN PREPARATION FOR THIS LESSON, BE SURE TO READ CHAPTER TEN IN THE BOOK, ***The Handwriting on the Wall.***

OVERVIEW

Under the fearful persecution of Nero, the Christians of Rome went through fiery trials. Multitudes of them were burned at the stake. The very streets at night were ghastly to behold because they were lit up with human torches made out of the Christians who were being burned alive.

In the Polish romance, *Quo Vadis,* Peter is shown fleeing the persecution with a little band of fugitive Christians. He comes face-to-face with Jesus, who was walking toward the city. The Lord said to Peter, "Where are you going?" Peter asked Him the same question, and the Lord said, "I'm going back to Rome to be crucified again because my servant Peter has turned his back on the cross." Peter answered, "Not so, Lord. I will go back and gladly die for thee."

Tradition tells us Peter let them nail him to the cross upside down so he would not be compared to his Lord, trusting that his blood would be the seed of the Church and his sacrifice would send the message of Truth farther than his living speech would carry it.

I don't know the truth of the first part of the story, but I do believe Peter was crucified upside down because he felt himself unworthy to be crucified in the same manner as his Lord. And as I read the story, I was reminded that the heritage of our faith is founded upon the sacrifice and courage of people like Peter and Daniel.

Daniel was wonderfully delivered from death. Peter paid for his faith with his life. Believing God does not necessarily guarantee that you will not be eaten by lions; but in Daniel's case, deliverance was part of God's plan.

Daniel Preferred by Darius

The Scripture records that when King Darius came into the Medo-Persian rule, he chose Daniel out of all the men in his kingdom and made him prime minister. He was one of three presidents, but he was above the other two. Under him were all of the 120 princes that governed throughout that great area. He was preferred "because an excellent spirit was in him" (Daniel 6:3). He had God within him.

Daniel Persecuted by His Enemies

Daniel had no sooner taken that responsibility when he was persecuted by his enemies. They determined to get Daniel. They were jealous and envious of him. He was a foreigner who had been elevated above them, and they hated him. He was also an honest man. They were not able to traffic in corruption as they were accustomed.

> "Daniel distinguishes himself from all the other authorities. . . . He is the wisest of the wise and the most capable of everyone in the land. . . . [Daniel's enemies] know that Daniel's religion is the fundamental guiding principle of his life. He would betray the king before he would betray his religion."
>
> Tremper Longman III, *Daniel, The NIV Application Commentary*

They tried first to indict him for some fault in his life, but they could find nothing wrong with him. In his professional life he was clean. In his personal life he was absolutely spotless. They determined the only way they could get Daniel in trouble was to accuse him in the matter of his religion. They observed that Daniel was diligent in his prayer life. So they determined to catch him in a habit they knew he would never break.

Daniel Persistent in His Testimony

When they passed the law that King Darius was to be god for a month and anybody who refused to bow down before him would be thrown into the den of lions, Daniel was caught in the trap. The king was actually the one caught because, when he agreed to the law, he didn't know Daniel would be the one condemned.

Daniel didn't change at all. He kept right on doing what he had always done. He persisted. In the text it says over and over that Daniel was a persistent man of God. In this passage, twice the king said to him, "Daniel, you are the guy who continually serves his God" (see 6:16, 20). That was his testimony. He persisted in his faith.

Daniel Protected by His God

The Displeasure of the King

When the king heard about Daniel disobeying the commandment and praying to his own God, the king was very displeased. He was not displeased with Daniel; he was displeased with himself because he had been tricked. He didn't want to hurt Daniel.

King Darius had his heart set on delivering Daniel. The Bible says he worked until the sun went down trying to find a way out for Daniel. But under Persian law, when a person was convicted of a crime and the sentence was passed, the sentence was carried out on that same day. As soon as the sentence was passed, there was no opportunity for redress or appeal (Daniel 6:14-15).

The Deliverance of Daniel to the Lions' Den

You have probably seen pictures of Daniel standing in the lions' den in quiet contemplation with two or three lions looking at him in awe. You might want to adjust your picture of what happened that night. We find out later on in the text that those who accused Daniel were thrown into the den, and they were devoured before they hit the floor. How many people were there? Over a hundred princes and others, plus their families. How many lions would it take to eat that many people before they hit the floor of the lions' den? A lot of lions!

> "CHARLES SPURGEON ONCE said that it was a good thing the lions didn't try to eat Daniel. They never would have enjoyed him because he was fifty percent grit and fifty percent backbone."
>
> DR. DAVID JEREMIAH, *The Handwriting on the Wall– Secrets from the Prophecies of Daniel*

One sermon described Daniel sliding to the floor of the den and the big lions bounding up, then stopping short. "The initial roars died away as they formed a solid phalanx and looked toward this man as he stood in their den within their easy reach. There was some snorting and a little whining, and some of them turned around and went back to their caverns." Two lion cubs and their mother came and lay beside Daniel "as though to give him warmth and protection in the chilly dungeon."[1]

The Distress of the King

When King Darius went back to his palace, he could not sleep or eat or be diverted (Daniel 6:18). They couldn't find any way for the king to get his mind off of his troubled heart about his friend in the lions' den. The king was not only losing a friend, but he was also losing his number one administrator for the whole kingdom. Even though Darius had not deliberately delivered Daniel to the lions' den, he was responsible because his own vanity had caused it to happen.

The Deliverance of Daniel in the Lions' Den

The king got up early the next morning and hurried to the den. In a lamenting voice, he cried out, "Daniel, servant of the living God, has your God, whom you serve continually, been able to deliver you from the lions?" (Daniel 6:20) Earlier when they had put Daniel in the lions' den, the king said to him, "Your God, whom you serve continually, He will deliver you" (verse 16). That's the kind of pious thing you say to someone who is hurting, even when you don't believe it yourself. Obviously the king didn't believe it because he asked if what he said had happened.

Daniel responded, "My God sent His angel and shut the lions' mouths, so that they have not hurt me" (verse 22). The rationale for his deliverance was that he was innocent.

The king reacted with gladness and commanded them to take Daniel out of the den. Daniel was not hurt at all, and the reason given for this in the Scripture was, "because he believed in his God" (verse 23).

The history of what God has done in a miraculous way from the beginning of Christianity right up to the modern day is wrapped up in what God does for somebody who believes in his God. It wasn't because Daniel was special. He wasn't one of God's pets. It wasn't because he was elected or foreordained or predestined. It was because Daniel believed in his God. He wasn't any different from us except in the measure of his faith in his Almighty God.

Daniel Proved by His God

Verse 24 is a sorry story of the paganism of the Medo-Persian Empire. It says, "And the king gave the command, and they brought those men who had accused Daniel, and they cast them into the den of lions—them, their children, and their wives; and the lions overpowered them, and broke all their bones in pieces before they ever came to the bottom of the den."

Sometimes people try to explain the story of Daniel by saying the lions weren't very hungry that day, or that Daniel hid and the lions couldn't find him. But these were hungry, ravenous, ferocious lions.

All of those who persecuted Daniel were themselves persecuted. I believe when people reach out to touch God's anointed, God often touches them.

Daniel and Practical Applications

The Probability of the Lions' Den

The nature of the Christian faith marks all of us for the lions. We are out of step with the world around us, and that's why we are always in jeopardy of the lions' den. Earlier in the book of Daniel, Shadrach, Meshach, and Abed-Nego were standing when everyone else was kneeling. Now everybody else is standing, and Daniel is kneeling. Shadrach, Meshach, and Abed-Nego were out of step with their times. Daniel was out of step with his times.

God delivered them. But He delivered them through the fiery furnace and through the lions' den. There was no attempt on the part of God to withhold them from the pressure of certain death. It will be like that for you and me. Suffering and testing are inevitable in the life of a Christian.

The Promise of the Lions' Den

Daniel was not kept from the lions, but he was kept in the midst of them. God has not promised to keep us from difficulty, but He has promised to keep us in the midst of it.

When I first began to travel, I had a very difficult time with it. I was afraid something would happen to me and I'd never see my family again. But one day I read this statement: "A man of God in the will of God is immortal until his work on earth is done." I don't worry anymore because if I'm in the will of God, going where God wants me to go, I'm all right. When God is done with me, I don't want to be around here anymore.

The Purpose of the Lions' Den

If God is a good God and in control, why would He ever let any of His children go through the kind of testing described in Daniel? God took the lions' den and used it for His glory and purpose. After the lions' den incident, King Darius made a decree that, "In every dominion of my kingdom men must tremble and fear before the God of Daniel. For He is the living God, and steadfast forever; His kingdom is the one which shall not be destroyed, and His dominion shall endure to the end. He delivers and rescues, and He works signs and wonders in heaven and on earth, who has delivered Daniel from the power of the lions" (Daniel 6:26-27). At the beginning of the chapter, we have a new regime. At the end of the chapter we have a new religion by the decree of the king who was touched by the power of the Almighty God.

The Prosperity of Daniel

The glory of God was the first purpose of the difficulties; the prosperity of Daniel was the second. Daniel prospered. The purpose of testing is to glorify God, but it is also to purify us. Whenever we are purified, we prosper. Whenever God puts us in the furnace and drains off all the dross, we come out as pure gold.

We may not be asked to face a den of lions, but God is asking us to live our life honestly before a watching world, unashamed to give testimony to our faith in Jesus Christ.

Note

1. Pastor Robert C. Stone. "A Character Study: Daniel—Another Look at the Lions' Den."

PERSONAL QUESTIONS

1. Read Daniel 6:14-23.

   a. Describe King Darius' dilemma between his new law and his friendship with Daniel.

   b. What was the king's goal after he found out he couldn't change the new law? (verse 14)

   c. How did the situation with Daniel impact the king physically and emotionally? (verses 14, 18)

   d. What was the first thing King Darius did the next day? (verse 19)

   e. How did God protect Daniel when he was thrown into the lions' den? (verse 22)

   f. Describe King Darius' reaction when he found out Daniel was still alive. (verse 23)

g. Why did God deliver Daniel from the lions' den?

h. How did Daniel respond to the king when he was rescued? (verses 21-22) Would you respond differently? If so, what would you say to the king?

2. Have you ever experienced a trial where you saw the reason for it later? If so, what happened?

a. How did you feel before you knew the reason for the trial?

b. How long did it take to understand the reason for the trial?

c. What did you learn about God through your trial?

GROUP QUESTIONS

1. Turn to Daniel 6:14-28 together.

   a. Discuss the dilemma King Darius created for himself. (verses 14-20)

   b. How do we know the king didn't believe God would deliver Daniel? (verses 16, 20)

   c. What was Daniel's condition when he was taken out of the lions' den? (verse 23)

   d. What happened to the men who accused Daniel of breaking the law? (verse 24)

   e. How did the men's actions affect their families? (verse 24)

f. What was King Darius' response to God's protection of Daniel? (verses 25-27)

g. How did the king describe God in his decree? (verses 26-27)

h. How was Daniel's life described after his time in the lions' den? (verse 28)

2. Share a lesson you learned during a trial in your own life.

   a. What did you learn about God during the trial?

b. Did you ever find out a purpose for the trial? If so, what was the purpose?

c. Did the outcome of your trial point others to God? If so, share how this happened.

DID YOU KNOW?

"The laws of the Medes and Persians" (see Daniel 6:8, 12, 15) is often used to refer to what was standard royal practice in the Persian Empire: Once the king had issued a decree, it could not be broken. The king, therefore, would be bound by his own decree, which is how Darius' advisors tricked him into sentencing Daniel to death. King Xerxes faced the same dilemma concerning the edict motivated by Haman to destroy the Jews in Persia. Esther asked the king to write a new decree rescinding the first one, allowing the Jews to be saved, a request Xerxes granted (see Esther 8). In effect, the only way a decree of a Persian king could be changed was by issuing a new decree overriding the first.

God's Animal Parade

Daniel 7:1-8

In this lesson we survey the outline of future world kingdoms given to Daniel.

OUTLINE

Critics of the Bible say that Daniel couldn't have been the author of the book of Daniel since no one can predict the future. But Daniel didn't predict the future world kingdoms, God did—and He gave the knowledge to Daniel in a dream that was perfectly accurate.

I. The Setting of Daniel's Dream

II. The Sequence of Daniel's Dream

A. The First Beast
B. The Second Beast
C. The Third Beast
D. The Fourth Beast
E. The Fifth Kingdom

III. The Schooling of Daniel's Dream

A. The Progress of Human History
B. The Preservation of Human History
C. The Purpose of Human History

In preparation for this lesson, be sure to read chapter eleven in the book, ***The Handwriting on the Wall.***

OVERVIEW

Professor Alfred Weber, a great historian, wrote in *Farewell to European History,* "To the one endowed with historical perspective, it must be clear that we are in the end of world history as we know it."

No matter how one reads history or ponders the prophecies of secular or religious prophets, we all recognize that strange things are happening in the world today. Unrest is almost everywhere in our world. It feels like war could break out at any time in four or five key spots around the globe. Self-destruction does not seem unlikely. What will be the final outcome of the nations in this period of history? Can anyone know? Yes, we can know. We cannot know all the details, but God has provided for us a broad scope of prophecy.

According to Dr. John Walvoord, former president of Dallas Theological Seminary, the seventh chapter of Daniel "provides the most comprehensive and detailed prophecy of future events that you will find anywhere in the Old Testament." But it is not a linear book. The message is not consecutive. The first six chapters of Daniel are a historic chronology. Chapters 7–12 are visions that took place during the period historically described in chapters 1–6.

Daniel's four dreams took place over a period of 22 years. In Daniel 1–6, Daniel interpreted dreams for others. In chapters 7–12, Daniel interpreted his own dreams. Chapter 2 is a dream given to Nebuchadnezzar and interpreted by Daniel. Chapter 7 is a dream given to Daniel and interpreted by an angel. Chapter 2 relates Nebuchadnezzar's viewpoint of history, the great accomplishments of humanity. Chapter 7 gives God's viewpoint of that same time—a bunch of ravenous beasts devouring one another.

The Setting of Daniel's Dream

Daniel is the first apocalyptic writer in the Bible. He wrote and conveyed prophetic truth by means of signs and symbols. He had a vision, and the symbols of his dream were threefold.

First of all, he saw a great sea. Four seas are generally mentioned in the Bible: the Galilean Sea, the Red Sea, the Dead Sea, and the Great Sea. The Great Sea was the Mediterranean. In his dream, Daniel was standing by the great Mediterranean Sea.

But there is also a figurative meaning to the word "sea." That is the great "sea of humanity."

The second thing Daniel saw in his dream was four winds blowing on that sea. The number four in the Bible often stands for the earth. We have the four winds from the four corners of the world, the four points of the compass, and the four seasons. In this passage, Daniel is picturing a gigantic sea with winds from all of the four points of the compass blowing in upon that sea. It is a picture of the world's condition. The striving of the wind upon the sea denotes political strife and uprisings, wars and bloodshed among the nations (verse 2).

> "NOW DANIEL WASN'T any different from you or me, except in the measure of his faith in his Almighty God. The history of what God has done in a miraculous way from the beginning of Christianity right up to the modern day is contained in what God does for somebody who believes in Him."
>
> DR. DAVID JEREMIAH, *The Handwriting on the Wall–Secrets from the Prophecies of Daniel*

The third thing Daniel saw was four great beasts coming out of the sea. In the ancient world, generally speaking, animals were used as symbols of kingdoms even as they are today. Today the lion represents Great Britain. The eagle represents the United States. Almost every nation has its own animal representative. These beasts coming up out of the sea were kingdoms that have existed in the world (verse 3).

THE SEQUENCE OF DANIEL'S DREAM

The words of sequence in verses 4-8 are very important. The beasts didn't all come up at the same time. They followed each other, one at a time. Each of these beasts represents a chronology of kingdoms exactly as in Daniel 2. The first, the head of gold, was Babylon. The second, the arms and the chest of silver, was Medo-Persia. The third, the belly of bronze, was Greece. And the fourth, the legs of iron, was Rome. The interpretation of chapter 7 will be of the same nations in the same sequence, only we will see it from God's viewpoint. As God looks at them, they are bestial—they are animals.

The First Beast

The first beast was like a lion that had eagle wings. The lion is the king of beasts, and the eagle is the king of birds. This animal symbolizes the Babylonian Empire which in Daniel 2 was symbolized by the head of gold. The head of gold has now become a lion in God's eyes.

The national symbol of Babylon was a winged lion. The wings indicate the swift conquest of a strong and cruel kingdom. This first beast combines the majesty of the lion and the strength and power of an eagle. In Jeremiah 49:19-22, the eagle and the lion are both used to describe Nebuchadnezzar. Daniel is very specific when he gives prophecies.

Daniel 7:4 says of the winged lion, "I watched till its wings were plucked off; and it was lifted up from the earth and made to stand on two feet like a man, and a man's heart was given to it." When Nebuchadnezzar was proud of his Babylonian Empire, God struck him down, and he became a beast. He walked on all fours and ate grass. That's kind of like being plucked.

Like Nebuchadnezzar at his return to sanity, the beast got up on two feet. The beast was even given a heart like a man. The beast out of the sea is the Babylonian Empire.

The Second Beast

The second animal is a bear (verse 5). Babylon fell to Medo-Persia. In keeping with the sequence in Daniel 2, the next kingdom is Medo-Persia.

There are thirteen references to bears in the Bible. Almost every time they are mentioned, they are cast in a context of ferocious, violent behavior. These bears have appetites that are never satisfied. This second kingdom was never satisfied until she reached from the Indus River on the east to the land of Egypt and the Aegean Sea on the west. God granted this second kingdom the authority to subjugate many nations like a greedy bear.

In the dream, there were three ribs in the mouth of the bear. Historians tell us that Medo-Persia conquered Lydia, Babylon, and Egypt. The ribs in the mouth of the bear were the victims of the previous hunt. Still the bear was not satisfied.

> "A TEACHER ONCE asked a Sunday school class if they thought Daniel was afraid, and one little girl answered, 'I don't think he was scared, 'cause one of the lions was the Lion of the tribe of Judah who was in there with him.' That child knew her Bible."
>
> DR. DAVID JEREMIAH, *The Handwriting on the Wall–Secrets from the Prophecies of Daniel*

Daniel also saw that the bear was lifted up on one side. I picture a circus bear doing a trick with two paws on one side held up. What was the meaning? In the Medo-Persian Empire, the Persians were dominant. By the end of the book of Daniel, the Medes were about gone. The Persians were in control.

The Third Beast

"After this I looked, and there was another, like a leopard, which had on its back four wings of a bird. The beast also had four heads, and dominion was given to it" (Daniel 7:6). The leopard represented Greece. It is known in the animal kingdom as swift, cunning, cruel, with an insatiable appetite for blood. This is in keeping with Daniel 2 and could be none other than the Greek Empire under Alexander the Great. History records that Persia was defeated by Greece. The four wings on the back of the leopard speak of the conquest and of its ability to strike fast.

This leopard had four heads. History tells us that after Alexander the Great died in 323 B.C., his kingdom was divided among his four generals—Ptolemy, Seleucus, Lysimachus, and Cassander. This fits the picture of the four-headed leopard.

The Scripture goes on to say dominion was given to him. With 35,000 soldiers, Alexander the Great went up against the Medo-Persian army of 200,000 to 300,000 soldiers and miraculously won. Everybody said it was the military strategy of Alexander the Great. But it was God who gave the dominion to him. Alexander was subject to a higher power. God is sovereign.

The Fourth Beast

Chapter 2 of Daniel says about Rome, "The fourth kingdom shall be as strong as iron, inasmuch as iron breaks in pieces and shatters everything; and like iron that crushes, that kingdom will break in pieces and crush all the others" (verse 40). This is the iron kingdom of Rome.

In the seventh chapter, the beast is described as "dreadful and terrible, exceedingly strong. It had huge iron teeth; it was devouring, breaking in pieces, and trampling the residue with its feet. It was different from all the beasts that were before it, and it had ten horns" (verse 7). There isn't any animal in the animal kingdom to which we can compare the fourth beast. There wasn't anything Daniel could describe when he saw this horrible beast representing the imperialistic and cruel materialism of Rome. Imperialistic Rome was known for her cruelty.

It was Rome that invented crucifixion. It was Rome that crucified Peter. It was Rome that beheaded Paul. It was Rome that banished John. It was Rome that burned the Christians. It was Rome that crucified our Lord. Truly it was different from all the beasts that were before it in its cruelty.

The ten horns are ten kingdoms who rule simultaneously. Among them one will appear who, conquering the others, will eventually dominate the entire empire and become the world dictator. We are talking here about the Antichrist. There has never been a ten-part Roman Empire, so this has to be future. Most prophetic scholars believe this part of the prophecy will be fulfilled in some kind of a revived Roman Empire, perhaps even something like the European Common Market.

The Fifth Kingdom

When we call this ten-part empire the fifth kingdom, we are not exactly accurate because these ten horns grow out of the head of the fourth beast. They are a last development of the fourth beast. This suggests that Rome was not destroyed nor did it disappear. Rome is the only kingdom that did not get conquered by a greater power. Rome did not die. She fell apart because of internal corruption and rottenness. The nations of Western Europe and those adjacent to the Mediterranean Sea are still geographically a part of what was once the Roman Empire. Nations that immigrated to Rome did not found a new kingdom but intermarried into the Roman families and continued the old Roman kingdom without dominion.

The Schooling of Daniel's Dream

The Progress of Human History

I think God is trying to teach us something in this passage about the progress of human history. Evolution in human history is not observable. Modern technological progress in no way invalidates what I have just said because it is international justice, peace, and human government that show national identity and security. These realms are hard to find as we study history in progress. Although man glories in the advances and achievements of civilization through the centuries, God clearly sees human history as a chronicle of immorality, brutality, and depravity. Government and its leaders may mask their true character from people for a time, but they are always unmasked before God.

Just as we have moved from the royal lion to the beast, as human history unfolds, it does not get better, it gets worse.

The Preservation of Human History

Another lesson is the preservation of human history. All of the secular prophets are prophesying that we won't last as a civilization much past the year 2000. God says that won't happen. While the civilization of the ten kingdoms is still intact, Jesus will come back. So the world will remain when Christ comes back.

The Purpose of Human History

The third lesson has to do with the purpose of human history. Why would God allow the kingdoms to get worse and worse, destroying and devouring each other? I think it is because God is giving humanity an opportunity to demonstrate how inept they are at trying to rule the world God created. All of the coups, plots, rebellions, and all of the chaos are reminders that what man has never been able to do, God in heaven has in control. And one day King Jesus is going to come and set it right.

PERSONAL QUESTIONS

1. Read Daniel 7:1-8.

   a. What were the three symbols Daniel saw in his dream? (verses 2-3)

   b. What sea is the "Great Sea" in verse 2? What is the figurative meaning of the word "sea" in this passage?

   c. Describe each of the four beasts in Daniel's vision. (verses 3-7)

   d. What kingdom does each beast represent?

   e. How is each beast an accurate description of its kingdom?

f. Why is the sequence of the dream important?

g. What made the little horn in verse 8 different from the other horns?

2. What did you learn about God's character in these verses?

a. How does God's sovereignty give you peace when you look at our world today?

b. What hope does this give you for the future?

GROUP QUESTIONS

1. Turn to Daniel 7:1-8 together.

   a. When do the dreams described in chapters 7–12 of Daniel take place in relation to the rest of the book of Daniel? Discuss why understanding the structure of the book of Daniel is an important part of studying Daniel's dreams.

   b. How did the first beast represent the Babylonian Empire? (verse 4)

   c. How did the bear represent Medo-Persia? (verse 5)

   d. Whom did the four heads of the leopard represent? (verse 6)

   e. How was the Roman Empire "dreadful and terrible, exceedingly strong"? (verses 7-8)

f. Discuss the fifth kingdom, which comes out of Rome.

1. Why is this a future kingdom?

2. How might this kingdom come into existence?

g. What is God's view of human history?

2. Have you ever thought about God at work in history?

a. Share how you can see Him at work in the rise and fall of past kingdoms.

b. Discuss why God allows kingdoms and governments to continue to become worse and worse throughout the ages.

DID YOU KNOW?

The fourth beast Daniel saw became the Roman Empire that was never conquered. Its remnants consist of the modern European and Mediterranean nations. Those nations are coalescing into something called the European Union (EU), currently with 28 member nations. It was created in 1993 on the foundations of prior European unity efforts and consists of a half-billion citizens who produce approximately 30 percent of the world's gross domestic product. The individual nations maintain some national rights and laws, while participating in other standards as a community of nations (like a unified currency, the Euro). The EU, in the eyes of many Bible students, is the structure that will likely give rise to a revived Roman Empire in the End Times.

ANCIENT OF DAYS

Daniel 7:9-14

In this lesson we discover the good news of the coming kingdom of God.

OUTLINE

In his vision of the beasts, Daniel could have been excused for having a pessimistic outlook—human kingdoms succeeding one another. But his vision was consummated with the sight of the Son of Man and the inauguration of His eternal kingdom on earth.

I. The Ancient of Days in Heaven
- A. His Eternity
- B. His Purity
- C. His Majesty
- D. His Authority
- E. His Deity

II. The Beast on Earth

III. The Son of Man in Heaven

IV. The Kingdom of Jesus Christ
- A. Unlimited
- B. Unique
- C. Unified
- D. Universal
- E. Unending
- F. Unconquerable

IN PREPARATION FOR THIS LESSON, BE SURE TO READ CHAPTER ELEVEN IN THE BOOK, ***The Handwriting on the Wall.***

OVERVIEW

David L. Cooper, in his studies on the book of Daniel, wrote that in order to understand Daniel's dream, you have to dream yourself. You need to imagine you are watching Daniel's vision on a motion picture screen. And the screen is split. There is a top section and a bottom section. The film begins in the first part of chapter 7 in the lower half of the screen, showing the beasts coming up out of the water, one at a time. When the terrible fourth beast is devouring the nations, the picture on the upper level suddenly comes alive. We see the Ancient of Days seated in the throne room of glory in heaven. On that divided screen, we see what is happening in heaven while we view the last gasp of the Roman Empire on earth.

One of the problems in studying and interpreting prophecy is that as the Old Testament prophets looked at the future, often it converged together for them. It would be like driving toward a mountain range and thinking there was one gigantic peak ahead of you. But when you got closer, you realized there was a great valley between the two peaks. Daniel, Isaiah, and Jeremiah looked to the future and saw the coming of Jesus Christ. They saw Him as coming to be born and coming to reign. But they did not know those would be two separate events, separated by many years.

An example of this is seen in Isaiah 61:1-2. "The Spirit of the Lord God is upon Me, because the Lord has anointed Me to preach good tidings to the poor; He has sent Me to heal the brokenhearted, to proclaim liberty to the captives, and the opening of the prison to those who are bound; to proclaim the acceptable year of the Lord, and the day of vengeance of our God." This is a prophecy concerning the first coming of Jesus to the earth. It lists the things Jesus would do when He came. But it adds, "The day of vengeance of our God"—a happening that is associated with His Second Coming. When Jesus read this passage in the synagogue to describe His earthly ministry at the time, He stopped before the line about vengeance, even though it was part of the sentence. He closed the book. Because that part of the prophecy would not happen for at least 1,900 years.

In Daniel 7, this same type of thing happens. Daniel was speaking about ancient kingdoms, then he mentioned the ten horns of the Roman Empire. That takes us to the time when the Lord will come again. Everything in this passage about the king and the

Antichrist and the Son of Man is removed from Daniel 7:7 by more than two thousand years.

The Ancient of Days in Heaven

This chapter is the only chapter in the Bible where the Ancient of Days is mentioned. He is mentioned here three times. It is the only passage in the Bible that pictures God in human form. He is not human. He is Spirit. But Daniel visualizes God as we would see God if we could understand what God would look like. He sees God the Father as the Ancient of Days. The term literally means, "the elderly One," "the One who has been around forever," "the One who never had a beginning." As he looks at God, he sees Him in His holiness, eternity, and glory. Almost all of the major attributes of God the Father are pictured in the scene that Daniel sees when he looks into heaven.

Here is the contrast. The bottom of the screen is turmoil, upheaval, chaos, beasts, and terrible things. The top half of the screen is the majestic throne room of glory with the Ancient of Days seated upon the throne.

His Eternity

The Bible describes Him first of all in His eternity. He is the Ancient of Days. He is the Source of time. He never had a beginning. He was never born. He is forever and forever.

His Purity

Next Daniel said, "His garment was white as snow" (Daniel 7:9). Usually when we see the term "white as snow" in the Bible, it is a picture of absolute purity. Daniel sees God the Father seated on His throne in absolute purity.

His Majesty

He also sees God in His majesty. God is seated on a throne, a throne that has been "put in place" (verse 9). It was put into position. God is the Sovereign Judge of the universe. He is about to judge the world.

His Authority

Next, we see Him in His authority. Daniel says, "His throne was a fiery flame, its wheels a burning fire" (verse 9). Many commentators believe the image of the fiery wheels pictures the possibility that the throne could go anywhere in the universe to bring judgment.

"A fiery stream issued and came forth from before Him" (verse 10). This is again a picture of the judgment of God. In all of the Bible, we are continually exposed to fire as a preparation for the judging God. It depicts God's presence.

His Deity

Finally in Daniel's vision, we see God's deity. "A thousand thousands ministered to Him; ten thousand times ten thousand stood before Him" (verse 10). This is not necessarily meant to be taken literally. It is a reminder to us of the tremendous number of angelic bodies that are before Him, bowing down and worshiping Him. He alone is worthy to be worshiped.

Then Daniel says, "And the books were opened" (verse 10). The judgment is about to begin. The written evidence is produced. God is about to judge the beastly nations of the world. The books are opened, and God is going to read the activity of the nations. He will read about their blasphemy and their idolatry and judge them guilty.

One commentator has written that in spite of all the different interpretations of this chapter, the chapter claims unambiguously that the Most High is reigning in heaven. His enemies think He is not in control, but He is in control all the same. He is the Sovereign God who rules and reigns. On the bottom half of the split screen, there is turmoil on earth. On the top half, the Ancient of Days is seated in the throne room of glory, opening the books. He is in control.

The Beast on Earth

Moving to Daniel 7:11-12, we are drawn back to the bottom half of the screen. Verses 11 and 12 tell us in rapid-fire description that the Beast was slain. Who is the Beast? The Beast is the Antichrist. He has risen up as a part of the fourth dynasty, his body is consumed in the fire, and the dramatic turn of events that takes place now is a picture of the sovereignty of our Divine Judge. The Beast will reign over the earth for three and a half years, and then he will be destroyed by the Supreme Judge of the whole world. Then he will be cast into the lake of fire.

Satan is not cast into the lake of fire until later. The first two to be thrown in are the Beast and the False Prophet (see Revelation 19:20). They are thrown in as God from heaven judges them guilty of sin and rebellion. The reign of terror of the Antichrist and the persecution of God's saints on earth have run their course. The Antichrist's cup of iniquity is full. Christ, whose name he has blasphemed and whose followers he has killed, consigns the Antichrist to the lake of fire, his final and proper doom.

The Son of Man in Heaven

In Daniel 7:13, we are finished with the events on earth, and we are back in heaven again. Daniel says, "I was watching in the night visions, and behold, One like the Son of Man, coming with the clouds of heaven! He came to the Ancient of Days, and they brought Him near before Him." We see the Son of Man in His human form. He has been given the privilege of judging the world. God the Father gave Him "dominion and glory and a kingdom, that all peoples, nations, and languages should serve Him. His dominion is an everlasting dominion, which shall not pass away, and His kingdom the one which shall not be destroyed" (verse 14). And He shall reign forever and forever.

The Kingdom of Jesus Christ

The kingdom of Jesus Christ superceded everything that happened on the bottom half of the screen, the kingdoms of humanity. In every way, it was better. In every way, it was greater.

Unlimited

In Daniel's description of the kingdom of Christ, we find that it is unlimited. The kingdoms of this world are throttled. Jesus Christ will be given dominion, all dominion without limitation. He will be the absolute monarch of the whole world.

Unique

We also find that the kingdom of Jesus Christ is unique, while the kingdoms of this world are typical. The Bible says there was given to Him dominion and glory. That's the difference in the kingdom of Jesus Christ. It's not a kingdom for its own sake. It is a kingdom for the glory of God. It's a kingdom filled with deity, a glorious kingdom. We have never seen anything like what God has in store when He sets up His kingdom.

> "When you see the Son in the air, when you see Him coming in the heavens, that's the sign that He is back. The Bible says He will come in a blaze of glory—the brilliant Son of God lighting up this darkened world. . . . And the sight will be so unbearably fearful that rebellious mankind will cry out for the rocks to fall on them, to hide their presence from the One who sits on the throne."
>
> Dr. David Jeremiah, *Signs of the Second Coming*

Unified

His kingdom is unified, while the kingdoms of this world are torn. The chaos and disruption and upheaval in the governments we see in Daniel didn't stop with the Roman Empire. It is going on today. In our world, human government is described by chaos; but when Christ comes back, He will rule a kingdom.

Universal

The kingdom of Jesus Christ is universal. The kingdoms of this world are territorial. The Bible says that His kingdom is over all people, and all nations, and all languages; and all of them are going to serve Him. Even the greatest kingdoms of Babylon and Rome and Greece, which were considered by historians to be worldwide kingdoms, did not cover all of the territory. But when Jesus comes to set up His kingdom, it is going to stretch from east to west to north to south. It will cover every little corner of the globe, and there will be no place where you can avoid the kingdom of God. Christ rules universally throughout the whole world.

Unending

The kingdom of our Lord is unending, while the kingdoms of this world are temporary. The Scripture says His dominion is everlasting, and it shall not pass away. Every king who came to authority thought he or his descendants after him would reign forever. Yet we have discovered that even the great Babylon, which seemed impregnable with its walls that were 387 feet high and 87 feet thick, one day fell. There was not a kingdom that ever survived like the kingdom of Jesus Christ—unending, forever and forever.

> **"ALEXANDER, CAESAR, CHARLEMAGNE and I have founded empires. But upon what did we rest the creation of our genius? Upon force. Jesus Christ founded His empire upon love, and at this hour millions of men would die for Him."**
>
> NAPOLEON BONAPARTE

Unconquerable

Finally, the kingdom of Jesus Christ is unconquerable, while the kingdoms of this world are triumphed over by each other. The Scripture says His kingdom shall not be destroyed. Who would destroy it? Who rivals King Jesus? Who can come and make a threat against the kingdom of our Lord and our God? There isn't anyone. It will never be destroyed.

What Daniel is trying to teach us is that what seems to be greatness in the kingdom of humans is nothing when compared with the greatness of the kingdom of Jesus Christ. When we see what God has in store for those who love Him, it helps us to understand what's going on in our world without becoming too upset.

As Christians there is a glad excitement for what will come when we have already experienced in some small way the kingdom of Christ in our hearts. Jesus took the fear out of what will happen at the Judgment by what He did on the cross. He made it possible for everyone to be an expectant anticipator of the coming of Christ if they will just put Him where He belongs—on the throne in their hearts.

PERSONAL QUESTIONS

1. Read Daniel 7:9-14.

   a. Describe the Ancient of Days. (verse 9)

   b. What attributes of God are represented in the description of the Ancient of Days?

   c. What does the description "white as snow" represent? (verse 9)

   d. How are the phrases "a thousand thousands" and "ten thousand times ten thousand" to be understood in verse 10?

   e. Who is the Beast mentioned in verse 11?

f. What happens to the Beast? (verse 11)

g. What is given to the Son of Man? (verse 14)

2. Explain how the split screen example helped explain the transition from verses 1-8 to verses 9-14.

   a. What was the top half of the screen showing? And the bottom half of the screen?

   b. Did this example help you visualize and understand the passage? If so, how did it do so?

GROUP QUESTIONS

1. Turn to Daniel 7:9-14 together.

   a. What do the fiery wheels and fiery stream coming from the Ancient of Days represent? (verses 9-10)

   b. How is the Ancient of Days' justice displayed in verse 11?

   c. Discuss the kingdom of Jesus Christ. (verse 14)

   d. How will the kingdom be unlimited and universal?

e. What makes the kingdom unique?

f. How do earthly kingdoms and governments fall short of the future kingdom of Jesus Christ?

g. Does a specific characteristic of Christ's kingdom give you hope? If so, share which one and why.

h. What do you most anticipate about life in Jesus' kingdom on earth?

i. Share why we as Christians can look at the world around us without becoming too upset at what is happening.

2. If applicable, share how the split screen example helped you understand the transition from verses 1-8 to verses 9-14.

DID YOU KNOW?

The phrase "Son of Man" (Daniel 7:13) is common in the Old Testament (107 times), used 93 times in Ezekiel alone. In the Old Testament, it was rarely a term for divinity, but most often referred to a prophet or other human being. In the four Gospels, however, the term is used exclusively to refer to Jesus as the Son of Man—the perfect human being prophesied in Daniel 7:13 who comes from God to set up His kingdom over the kingdoms of this world. The term is found only four times in the rest of the New Testament—once in Acts 7:56, once in Hebrews 2:6, and twice in the apocalyptic language of Revelation (1:13; 14:14) referring to Christ.

THE ANTICHRIST

Daniel 7:15-28

In this lesson we discover the identity of the imposing horn on the fourth beast in Daniel's vision—the coming Antichrist.

OUTLINE

The idea of a single individual gaining sway over the nations of the world is not as far-fetched an idea today as it once was—the earth is a "shrinking" planet with ever-increasing needs. The Bible makes it clear that such a leader will rise on the world's stage.

I. The Antichrist Will Be a Charismatic Leader

II. The Antichrist Will Be a Clever Leader

III. The Antichrist Will Be a Cultic Leader
- A. He Will Change the Times
- B. He Will Change the Laws
- C. He Will Do Great Things

IV. The Antichrist Will Be a Cruel Leader

V. The Antichrist and Us
- A. The Stage Is Being Set
- B. The Strategy of the Christian
- C. The Spirit of the Antichrist

IN PREPARATION FOR THIS LESSON, BE SURE TO READ CHAPTER TWELVE IN THE BOOK, ***The Handwriting on the Wall.***

OVERVIEW

One of the most popular indoor sports of theologians is trying to identify the Antichrist spoken of by Daniel and John. Everyone and everything from individual Roman rulers to the whole Catholic system, from the pope to Oliver Cromwell, from Hitler to John F. Kennedy, from Henry Kissinger to Judas Iscariot have been made candidates for the Antichrist.

In Revelation 13:18, we are told the number of the Antichrist is 666. People have tried to figure out who the Antichrist is by playing number games. The fun thing is that anyone can be the Antichrist if you do it right. You only have to follow three simple rules. One, if the proper name doesn't work, add a title. Two, if it doesn't work in English, try Hebrew, Greek, or Latin. Three, if none of those things work, cheat on the spelling.

Nobody knows what the number means. We won't know what it means until God wants us to know. We don't know who the Antichrist is, but we can know what he is. The Bible says he is more than just an insignificant person who will appear sometime in the future. There is a lot of information about him in the Bible. The seventh chapter of Daniel sets the stage for our understanding of the prophetic phenomena. It reminds us that the sovereign God is in control, and He takes us through the steps of human government. From the time of Daniel the prophet and the Babylonian kingdom to the end of human government when Christ the King returns, God gives us the whole scheme of things. Into that scheme, this individual fits.

> "WHILE WE DON'T know exactly how he will do it, [the Antichrist] will apparently be a political and diplomatic genius. Daniel 9 tells us that many are killed as a result of a covenant of 'peace' he makes with Israel. So under the guise of peace he elevates himself over the kingdoms of this world."
>
> DR. DAVID JEREMIAH, *Escape the Coming Night*

In the seventh chapter of Daniel, there are signposts that help you see the epics. These are the phrases used when Daniel says he saw a vision by night, or a night vision. There are three of these. The first begins Daniel's presentation of three great kingdoms of the world (see verse 2). The second begins Daniel's vision of the fourth kingdom over which Christ will be victorious (see verse 7). The third introduces the final chapter when Christ comes to reign on earth (see verse 13).

The Antichrist fits into the last part of that second epic. At the end of the final form of the final kingdom, the Bible says a man will arise to take leadership over it. That is the Antichrist.

The Antichrist Will Be a Charismatic Leader

The world is ripe for a leader who will come upon the stage of our world scene and command the respect and following of the world because nobody seems to have the answer to our international problems. All the world is looking for someone to solve them. When the Antichrist comes and by supernatural revelation begins to demonstrate that he has the ability to lead the world, they will be so anxious to see him come, they will fall down at his feet. The vacuum has been created.

People will be hungry for someone to follow. The Antichrist will be that type of person. He will be a charismatic leader. I don't mean he will be a Pentecostal. He will be a man with great charisma.

He will be a tremendous public speaker. Daniel 7:8 says he has "a mouth speaking pompous words." Verse 20 echoes that, and verse 25 says, "He shall speak pompous words against the Most High." Later on, when the Antichrist establishes a great image that everyone is supposed to worship, even the image will speak. Some think he will do it through ventriloquism; some think it will be demon possession. I don't know how he will do it, but this man will have great oratorical power.

Some have said the Antichrist will be noted for wonderful eloquence. He will be able to capture the attention and admiration of the world. He will be able to move the masses. Some have said he will be like Melanchthon, William Jennings Bryan, and Gladstone all wrapped up in one. Everyone who hears him speak will be caught up in his charisma as a great speaker. He will be able to weld these masses into activity, and the people will follow him.

The Bible also says there will be something about him that is attractive. It says of him, his "appearance was greater than his fellows" (Daniel 7:20). The word used here means, "abundant in size, in rank." Sometimes in the Bible it has to do with being a captain or chief or lord. It is a man of high rank or impressive appearance, like Saul in the Old Testament, who was head and shoulders above his fellows. This man, when he walks into the presence of others, will immediately capture their attention. Something about his very person will attract people, by an inhuman magnetism, to follow him.

The Antichrist Will Be a Clever Leader

This man will be the master politician of all history, the greatest diplomat who ever lived. Verse 20 says he has eyes. That phrase references his mental ability, his intellect, and his cleverness. He will be able to solve the problems of the world with his cleverness and wisdom. This is illustrated in verse 8. It says he will rise up at the time of the ten-king confederation and subdue three other kings. It describes it graphically, saying the three horns were "plucked out by the roots." This phrase means literally "to squeeze out, to push out by subterfuge, to come in and cleverly replace."

Daniel 11:21 is another illustration of his cleverness. "And in his place shall arise a vile person, to whom they will not give the honor of royalty; but he shall come in peaceably, and seize the kingdom by intrigue." The Antichrist will be the master of malarkey. He'll be able to talk people into anything.

The Antichrist Will Be a Cultic Leader

He Will Change the Times

The Antichrist will not just be in the political realm, he will also be in the realm of religion. He is a cultic leader. Daniel 7:25 says about him, "He shall speak pompous words against the Most High, shall persecute the saints of the Most High, and shall intend to change times and law." The Bible says he will stand up with his oratory and give great speeches against the Most High God.

Then he will put himself in God's place. He will ask people to fall down and worship him. One of the people later on in the book of Daniel is a historical type of the Antichrist. His name was Antiochus Epiphanes IV. He illustrates this concept of the Antichrist's self-worship. On the coins that survive from that day can be seen the figure of Zeus, whose features closely resemble those of Antiochus Epiphanes. One of those coins, which is now in the British Museum, has this inscription on it: "King Antiochus, God Manifest, Victory Bearer."

He Will Change the Laws

In his cultic leadership, the Antichrist will try to change the moral and natural laws of the universe. Verse 25 says he "shall intend to change times." Most people believe that means he will mess around with the calendar. He will do away with religious feast days. Some think he may try to get rid of the seven-day week, which is God-ordained time, and change it to a ten-day week like Napoleon tried to do during the French Revolution. The Antichrist will try to strip down everything that has anything to do with structure, anything that has to do with history and stability as far as religious beliefs are concerned. He'll take it away and start over from scratch. He will start his own religion to obliterate God from the picture.

The Bible says he will change the law. He will create his own morality. He'll say, "You don't have to follow the morality of God. Here is a new set of laws."

He Will Do Great Things

He will also be able to do great things. How could a man like the Antichrist be able to get enough people to follow him so he could rule the world? Second Thessalonians 2:9 tells us he will be equipped by Satan to do great wonders and great lies and great signs. He will heal. I believe he'll bring people back from the grave—at least give the appearance of it. He will be able to do things this world hasn't seen done since Jesus walked on the earth.

The Antichrist Will Be a Cruel Leader

The fourth beast "shall devour the whole earth, trample it and break it in pieces" (Daniel 7:23). He "shall persecute the saints of the Most High" (verse 25). Literally, he will wear them out. The people who are saved during the Tribulation period will become the targets of this man. He determines to destroy them. The believers' lives will be difficult, particularly after the

> **"If ever there was a word for these times as we begin a new millennium, it is deception. Our Lord's warning about deception (Matthew 24:4) ought to be etched on our hearts. While we must always be on the alert for deception, the Lord Jesus declares that we must be especially watchful for spiritual deceit as the day of His return approaches."**
>
> Dr. David Jeremiah, *Jesus' Final Warning*

Antichrist comes into full power during the last half of the Tribulation. He will harass and afflict and persecute them without mercy. Many of them will be martyred for their faith.

The phrase "to wear out the saints" is a phrase that comes out of the context of wearing out garments. It's not that he will come and just snuff them out. He will wear them out like you wear out clothes. He will harass them every minute, and he won't let them breathe.

He will probably wear them out through public seizure and through economic squeeze. We know about the mark on the head and on the hand. He'll starve some of them out. Antiochus Epiphanes, the first person recorded in history to persecute a people exclusively for their religious faith, caught a group of Jews in a cave observing the Sabbath. He had the mouth of the cave sealed and fires set inside to suffocate them. That's just one example of Antichrist behavior.

The Antichrist and Us

The Stage Is Being Set

The stage is already being set for the coming of the Antichrist. How? The abject conditions of the economy in Germany after World War I helped to catapult Adolph Hitler into power. The German treasury was low in gold. The budget was unbalanced. Sound familiar? Inflation went out of perspective. In 1919 the German mark was worth 25 cents. Within four years, it declined in value until four trillion were needed to equal one dollar in buying power. The German middle class lost all their savings. The value of every pension was wiped out. All security was gone. The people were ready to listen to any demi-god who would help them solve their bitterness. Enter Hitler.

It was Lenin who said, "The surest way to overthrow an existing social order is to debauch the currency." What do you think would happen in the United States if a charismatic wonder-working leader were to walk across the American scene and say to us, "I have the answer to the economic stress of this country"? The stage is being set for the arrival of a man like the man we've been talking about.

The Strategy of the Christian

The strategy of the Christian is not to look for the Antichrist. No place in the Bible does it say your job as a Christian is to look for the Antichrist. But we are to look for Christ appearing again.

When we see things that signal He will be appearing soon, our attention should refocus on the One who is coming—Jesus Christ, the coming King and Savior of all humanity. The Antichrist might be alive today, but speculation about him doesn't fit either of the two things God has told us we are to do in light of the coming of Christ. Those two things are to work and to watch.

The Spirit of the Antichrist

Another thing that puts this in perspective is the Bible's statement that the Antichrist is already here. In the book of 1 John we are told, "Every spirit that does not confess that Jesus Christ has come in the flesh is not of God. And this is the spirit of the Antichrist, which you have heard was coming, and is now already in the world" (1 John 4:3). The spirit of the Antichrist is everywhere in the world today.

What should we do? Be aware. And know that God has all of this in control. He has a plan that includes us, but not together with the Antichrist. Someday soon we are going to hear the shout, the trumpet will sound, and we are going to be caught up to meet Jesus Christ.

PERSONAL QUESTIONS

1. Read Daniel 7:15-28.

   a. What part of the vision did Daniel want to know about in more detail? (verse 19)

   b. Describe the Beast. (verses 19-25)

   c. What will draw people to the Beast?

   d. What will the Beast do against the Most High? (verse 25)

e. How will the Beast cause problems for those who become believers during the Tribulation? (verse 25)

f. What will the Beast change in the world? (verse 25)

g. To whom does the kingdom ultimately belong? (verse 27)

2. Have you ever speculated or heard others speculate about who the Beast (the Antichrist) is?

   a. If so, who did others or yourself speculate the Beast is?

   b. How did this passage describing the Beast help you understand more of the "what" of the Antichrist?

GROUP QUESTIONS

1. Turn to Daniel 7:15-28 together.

   a. Discuss the Beast and what he will do while he is in power on the earth.

   b. Who was a historical type of Antichrist later in Daniel? How did he illustrate the concept of self-worship?

   c. When and for how long will the Beast be in power on the earth?

d. What hope can we find in verses 26-27?

e. How did Daniel feel after the vision? (verse 28)

f. What was Daniel's response to the vision? (verse 28) What can we learn from Daniel's response?

2. Share who you or others have speculated about who the Beast (the Antichrist) is.

a. How did this passage describing the Beast help you understand more of the "what" of the Antichrist?

b. Why should our focus be less on who the Beast will be and more on what he will do?

3. Discuss what we are to be doing while waiting for Christ's return.

a. Share some practical ways we can accomplish these two tasks.

b. What action will you take to watch or wait well this week?

DID YOU KNOW?

The Greek prefix *anti* (on Antichrist) can mean "against" or "instead of." Therefore, the coming Antichrist may be one who opposes Christ or who tries to usurp Christ's position as God in the flesh. The term "Antichrist" occurs only in the letters of John (1 John 2:18, 22; 4:3; 2 John 7), but references to him abound in Scripture under other names. In 2 Thessalonians 2:3 Paul refers to him as "the man of sin . . . , the son of perdition." In the next verse, he incorporates both senses of *anti:* "who opposes and exalts himself above all that is called God or that is worshiped, so that he sits as God in the temple of God, showing himself that he is God."

THE REIGN OF TERROR

Daniel 7:15-28

In this lesson we learn how the Antichrist will attempt to subdue the earth and establish himself as ruler of mankind.

OUTLINE

Even though the Bible is clear about the Antichrist's rise on the world stage, when it happens it will seem normal and natural, not terrible. He will take advantage of people's fears and present himself as a savior before unleashing a reign of terror on the world.

I. The Appearance of the Antichrist
  A. His Inconspicuous Beginning
  B. His Intimidating Bearing

II. The Acclaim of the Antichrist
  A. The Cause of His Acclaim
  B. The Character of His Acclaim

III. The Authority of the Antichrist

IN PREPARATION FOR THIS LESSON, BE SURE TO READ CHAPTER TWELVE IN THE BOOK, ***The Handwriting on the Wall.***

OVERVIEW

Why study prophecy? If you are committed to the exposition of Scripture, you don't really have a choice. The Bible is one-fifth prophecy. Of the one-fifth that is prophetic, one-third concerns the Second Coming of Jesus Christ and the events that surround the Second Coming.

Next to faith, there is no subject in the Bible that is discussed more than the Second Coming of Jesus Christ. For every time His first coming is mentioned, His Second Coming is mentioned eight times. For every time the subject of atonement is mentioned, the Second Coming is mentioned twice. The Lord Himself refers to His coming again 21 times in His own words. And more than fifty times in the New Testament we are told to be ready for the coming again of the Lord Jesus Christ.

In the Old Testament, the book of Daniel is the key to understanding the Scriptures. In the New Testament, the book of Revelation is the key to understanding the Scriptures. Daniel prefigures Revelation, and Revelation interprets Daniel. The two taken together outline the scheme of events for the future which, when studied, gives any Bible student a map to chart the course of events for our day.

The Appearance of the Antichrist

His Inconspicuous Beginning

First of all, note his inconspicuous beginning. Daniel 7:7 speaks of ten horns that grow up as a part of the final form of the Roman Empire. Those ten horns remind us of the ten-kingdom confederation that will be a part of the final form of the Roman Empire, which will reign upon the earth in the End Times. In the ten-horn prophecy, there is a reference to an eleventh horn, a "little horn." It is an inconspicuous kingdom or king in light of the other great kings. That little horn is a reference to the Antichrist. He is the one who is insignificant in his beginning but who grows to be the king of the earth.

In Revelation 13:1, we read that this first beast with seven heads and ten horns and ten crowns upon his heads and the name of blasphemy written on him comes up out of the sea. The word "sea" in prophetic Scripture is always a reference to masses of people. This reference means that the Antichrist rises out of multitudes of people of his day. He is not brought dramatically before the world and announced, but he inconspicuously begins his ministry behind the scenes before he is finally brought out to center stage.

1. Politically

> "WE CANNOT LEAVE Daniel 7 without attention to the picture of hope in the midst of the chaos. A 'son of man' rides a cloud to the rescue of those who are oppressed by the beastly human kingdoms. . . . Only God rides the ethereal war chariot. . . . Jesus is the divine warrior who will defeat the beast, the forces of evil at the end of time."
>
> TREMPER LONGMAN III, *The NIV Application Commentary*

We can learn something from Revelation 13 in a number of categories. First of all, politically. The Scripture says the Antichrist is out of the sea. Not only does the sea signify the great masses of people, but it is also a reference to the turmoil that will reign in the End Times. Isaiah the prophet speaks of the wicked, saying, "But the wicked are like the troubled sea, when it cannot rest, whose waters cast up mire and dirt" (Isaiah 57:20). The Bible says in the End Times there will be wars and rumors of wars. There will be chaos reigning. There will be turmoil politically. There will be lack of any organization or political direction. Out of that turmoil will arise this leader.

2. Nationally

As we study the personality of the Antichrist, we often run into people who want to consign him to a Jewish heritage. They say he must be a Jew because he makes a covenant with the Jewish people. That covenant indicates they consider him to be the Messiah, and no Jew would ever consider a non-Jew to be the Messiah. But the Bible does not teach that the league of the Antichrist with the Jewish nation is based on their idea that he is the Messiah. It is simply a political maneuver on his part to gain control over Israel, the center of military power.

The Bible does say the Antichrist arises out of the fourth empire, the Roman Empire. He comes out of the great empire that is reigning in the Last Days.

3. Spiritually

Revelation 11:7 says, "When they finish their testimony, the beast that ascends out of the bottomless pit will make war against them, overcome them, and kill them." The Antichrist will arise out of the abyss or pit. He is nothing more than Satan incarnate. He is a demon with a body. He is Satan walking around in the flesh. Satan has always been the great imitator. Just as God was incarnated in Jesus Christ and was God embodied, so Satan will determine to do the very same thing. He will embody himself in the Antichrist.

4. Providentially

Sometimes if you get a good picture of this evil person, it can keep you awake at night. We may wonder if, at the end of time, everything is going to run wild and God is going to lose control. But in Revelation 13, six different times it says that control was given to him. That is a reference not only to the fact that Satan controls the Antichrist, but it is also a reference to the fact that behind it all, the sovereign hand of God is keeping it all in control. He is the One who allows it, though He does not cause it. And it never, ever moves out of the range of His controlling hand and power. He is providentially and sovereignly in control.

His Intimidating Bearing

The Antichrist is an intimidator by his very appearance. He is described as "a beast rising up out of the sea, having seven heads and ten horns" (Revelation 13:1). The heads are covered with the names of blasphemy. He is a terrible creature. In total appearance, the Beast was like a leopard, his feet like those of a bear, and his mouth like a lion. All three characteristics of the three previous kingdoms (see Daniel 7:4-7) are embodied in the fourth kingdom, and in its final form in the Antichrist.

Whatever the Babylonian or the Medo-Persian or the Grecian empires had of strength and brutality and swiftness will be in the final form of the world rule of the western confederation of nations—the revived Roman Empire. That final nation or kingdom will have all of the parts of the previous kingdoms embodied in the kingdom and in the king.

He will be a composite of everything that will have happened up to that time. He will be Satan's masterpiece, the best Satan can do. This Antichrist will be the epitome of Satan's desire wrapped up in one person. No wonder he is such an awful person and such a frightening personality.

The Acclaim of the Antichrist

The Cause of His Acclaim

Revelation 13:3 says, "I saw one of his heads as if it had been mortally wounded, and his deadly wound was healed. And all the world marveled and followed the beast." One of the heads of the Beast was wounded to death. Here again is Satan's counterfeiting activity. Jesus Christ came to the cross and died and was buried and resurrected. The resurrection power of Christ was the trust which threw the Church into growth and tremendous spiritual renewal. Satan realizes if he is going to get the acclaim of the people, he'll need to do what God did. So he will get the Beast killed—or the appearance of being killed—then bring him back to life. His resurrection will cause his great following by all of the peoples in the nations of the world, except those whose names are written in the Lamb's Book. Everyone else will fall down and worship the Beast.

Years ago there were some who thought John F. Kennedy was the Antichrist because he was killed through a wound in the head. While he was lying in state in the Rotunda, there were many who thought Kennedy would revive, get up out of the coffin and become the leader of the world. That didn't happen. But think for a moment what you would have felt in your own heart and mind if you had been watching TV, seeing the endless parade before the casket, and suddenly John F. Kennedy got up, took the mic in his hand, and began talking to America.

The Character of His Acclaim

The Bible says something like this is going to happen with the Antichrist. He will receive a wound in his head. He will miraculously revive, and, as a result, people will follow him.

Not only that, they will worship him. Their worship will be based on two fundamental facts: his uniqueness and his great military exploits. They will be saying, "Who is like the beast? Who is able to make war with him?" (Revelation 13:4) Nobody will be able to stand up against him. He will be a conqueror wherever he goes.

The Authority of the Antichrist

Once the Antichrist has brought together three nations out of the European confederacy and gains control over them, then he will gain control over the ten confederate nations. After that, realizing he needs to deal with the Jews, he will go to Israel and make a covenant with the Jewish people. The covenant will allow them to continue their worship and temple practices. He will support them and protect them until three and a half years pass. Then he will walk into the temple and desecrate it, taking their worship away and causing all-out war between himself and the Jews. The Bible says that during this reign he will kill the two witnesses God sent to earth. He will corrupt the name of God and the people of God and take hold of a three-fold program that he will believe gives him absolute control in the world.

> "THE ANTICHRIST MIGHT be alive today, and he might be strutting on the stage of politics at this time, but speculation about him does not fit either of the two things God has told us to do in light of the coming of Christ: work (Luke 19:13) and watch (Matthew 25:13)."
>
> DR. DAVID JEREMIAH
> *The Handwriting on the Wall–Secrets from the Prophecies of Daniel*

The program is first of all religious. He is a blasphemer. Secondly, it is political. He is a military man. Thirdly, it is economic. He puts the "mark" on the people, and it's their credit card. If you don't have one, you can't buy and sell. He is the absolute ruler over the economy. He has everybody just where he wants them.

The authority of the Antichrist extends to all people—all except those who are written in the Book of Life. Everyone is under his control.

Revelation 13:9 tells us something important is going to happen now. Verse 9 is an exclamation point. It says, "Attention everybody. If you miss everything else in this chapter, don't miss verse 9 and what follows."

Revelation 13:9 says, "If anyone has an ear, let him hear." Then verse 10 says, "He who leads into captivity shall go into captivity; he who kills with the sword must be killed with the sword. Here is the patience and the faith of the saints." It's saying that though the reign of the Antichrist is worldwide and his dominion without peer, his end is in sight! The Antichrist will reign for a time, but then he will be destroyed.

If you study the book of Revelation, you can find his end right in that book. The Bible says the Antichrist and his followers will come to war with Jesus Christ and His followers, and the Lamb will overcome. Then in Revelation 19:20, you see the Beast cast into the lake of fire burning with brimstone, along with the False Prophet. When the devil is thrown into the lake of fire, the other two are still there (see Revelation 20:10).

It's tremendous to know all about this, but it would be frightening if we didn't have the last chapter. God, by the Spirit, has given us the last chapter. He says to us who read it that the Antichrist, who is the best Satan has to offer, is going to reign for a time, but it is limited. His end is in sight. The King will come and set up His eternal reign and dominion. And He shall reign forever and ever.

The thing I get so excited about when I study this prophecy is that I am on the winning side. I know all about the fight, but I know who's going to win, and I have cast my lot with the King of Kings.

PERSONAL QUESTIONS

1. Have you thought about the importance of studying prophecy? If so, why do you think it is important to study prophecy?

2. Read Daniel 7:15-28.

   a. How does the Antichrist begin his ministry?

   b. How will the political climate make it easy for him to rise to power?

   c. Where will the Antichrist come from?

d. Describe Satan's influence on and control of the Antichrist.

e. What will happen to the Antichrist that will cause people to follow him?

f. What is the three-part program the Antichrist will implement to give himself control of the entire world?

g. How will the Antichrist have control over the economy?

3. Describe how God's sovereignty is displayed at the end of the Antichrist's reign.

   a. Have you experienced a situation where God's sovereignty was evident after a fearful or difficult time?

   b. If so, describe the situation and how God used it to strengthen your faith.

GROUP QUESTIONS

1. Discuss the importance of studying prophecy.

    a. How does Scripture show us the importance of prophecy?

    b. How do the books of Daniel and Revelation help us understand Scripture?

2. Turn to Daniel 7:15-28.

    a. Discuss the Antichrist's relationship with Israel.

b. What is his initial relationship with them?

c. What will change in this relationship after three and a half years?

d. What does the Antichrist do that causes a change in the relationship?

e. What wording in verses 25-26 indicates who is in charge of the Antichrist's power?

3. If applicable, share how God's sovereignty was evident to you after a fearful or difficult situation in your life. Share how God used this time to strengthen your faith.

DID YOU KNOW?

Before the current European Union alliance of 28 nations, there was the European Common Market. At one time there were ten nations as members, and many believed this might be the foundation of the "ten horns" on the beast in Daniel 7, representing the revival of the fourth beast—the revived Roman Empire. But the European alliance continued to grow beyond ten. There are currently 28 nations in the EU. But Daniel 7:24 does not say the ten horns represent ten nations, but ten kings. So regardless of how many countries are bound together, there will be ten leading figures, overshadowed by an eleventh (the Antichrist; verses 24-25) who will rise in authority.

The Church and the Tribulation

Selected Scriptures

In this lesson we learn the contents and meaning of Daniel's second vision.

OUTLINE

Many who read the descriptions of life during the Tribulation wonder if we are not already in it, so dire do world circumstances appear. The answer is "No"—the Tribulation will not begin until the Church of Jesus Christ has been removed from earth.

- **I. Definition of the Tribulation**
  - A. Reasons
  - B. Revelation
- **II. Dependence on Consistent Interpretation**
- **III. Discussion of the Tribulation Period**
- **IV. Deliverance Promise**
- **V. Doctrine of Imminency**

In preparation for this lesson, be sure to read chapter five in the book, ***The Handwriting on the Wall.***

OVERVIEW

In the study of prophecy, there are four different views about the Tribulation period. First there is the Post-Tribulational view. This view teaches that the Church will go through seven years of Tribulation and when it is over, the Church will be raptured and taken home to be with the Lord.

Another view is called the Mid-Tribulation rapture position. This view teaches that at the end of three and a half years the Church is raptured and not here for the next three and a half years of the Tribulation.

The view I believe, according to our creeds and doctrinal statement, is the Pre-Tribulation rapture. This view teaches that before the Tribulation starts, the Church will be raptured and taken away from here.

There is one other view called the partial rapture view. A man named Witness Lee teaches that only those believers who are spiritual will be raptured when the Lord comes back. The rest of the Church will have to go through the Tribulation. It's kind of a Protestant purgatory.

There isn't any evidence in the Word of God that such a thing will happen. The Bible teaches the unity of the Body. God isn't going to have part of the Body up there while the rest of the Body is down here. The Church will be caught up together to be with the Lord. Another problem with the partial rapture theory is that it says our works determine in some respect how we escape punitive judgment. That isn't consistent with the Bible.

We believe in the Pre-Tribulational rapture position simply because of what the Bible teaches us about the nature of our Christian faith. The Bible teaches that the moment a person believes in Jesus Christ, he passes out of death into life and there is no condemnation hanging over him. Those who believe in Post-Tribulationism believe there is condemnation hanging over them which they will experience for seven years on this earth.

Definition of the Tribulation

The Tribulation period in the Bible is defined as the final period of Jehovah's determined dealings with Daniel's people in order to finish Israel's transgressions. There are two reasons for the Tribulation period.

Reasons

First of all, it is to purge out the Jewish rebels. Second, it is to punish Gentile rejecters. The Bible teaches that during the seven year period of time, the wrath of God is going to come primarily upon the Jews, but even the Gentiles who have rejected Christ during that time will be objects of the wrath of God.

Revelation

The definition of the Tribulation period is given to us in great detail in the book of Revelation. Revelation is a self-interpreting book. It is a book that tells you what the signs are, then what those signs mean. At the beginning of the book, there is an outline right in the text (see Revelation 1:19). The outline is three-fold: the things John saw, the things which are, and the things which will be thereafter.

Revelation 1:1-20 is the record of what John saw when he was on the Isle of Patmos. That is the first subject on the outline. Chapters 2 and 3 deal with the seven churches of Revelation. That is the second subject, the things which are. Beginning at chapter 4 to the end of Revelation is the third subject, "the things which will take place after this" (Revelation 1:19).

Beginning at Revelation 4 through the nineteenth chapter, almost all of the information has to do with the period we know as the Tribulation. In that section of Scripture are the vials and judgments, bowls, trumpets and seals that picture the pouring out of God's wrath on this earth. The word "church" appears nineteen times in Revelation 1–3. It is not mentioned once as being on earth in chapters 4–19. During the time of Tribulation in Revelation, the Church is not mentioned one time. Why? Because the Tribulation will be going on down here on earth when the Church is up there with God. The Church will not be present at the Tribulation, so there is no reason to mention it.

> **"Two additional reasons the church must be in heaven during the Tribulation: The Judgment Seat of Christ must take place along with the Marriage Supper of the Lamb. If we are not raptured to be with the Lord until the end of the Tribulation, these two events cannot take place at the time Scripture seems to indicate they will."**
>
> Dr. David Jeremiah,
> *Escape the Coming Night– A Message of Hope in a Time of Crisis*

Dependence on Consistent Interpretation

The doctrine of Pre-Tribulation is not dependent on one passage of Scripture but on the consistent interpretation of all passages of Scripture where the truth is mentioned. Let's look first at 2 Thessalonians.

The believers in Thessalonica thought the Tribulation period had already started and they were living in the midst of it. Paul wrote the second letter to the Thessalonians first of all to tell them they were not in the Tribulation. He also wrote to answer their question, "Was Paul right when he taught that we would not go through the Tribulation?"

Paul lists the things that must happen before the Tribulation can happen. He says first of all, "That Day will not come unless the falling away comes first" (2 Thessalonians 2:3). The phrase "falling away" is literally "apostasy." Most Bible students understand that word to mean the Tribulation period will follow hard on the heels of a time when the Church at large leaves the faith. It is a time of tremendous declension within the Church.

The second thing that must happen is "the man of sin is revealed, the son of perdition" (verse 3). The Tribulation period will not come in full force until the falling away and the revelation of the man of sin, the Antichrist.

> "Millions upon millions of copies of the Bible and Bible portions have been published in all major languages and distributed throughout the world.... Removal of believers from the world at the Rapture will not remove the Scriptures, and multitudes will no doubt be constrained to read the Bible in those days ... [and] give their testimony for the Word of God."
>
> Dr. Henry Morris, cited in *Escape the Coming Night*

The third thing is in 2 Thessalonians 2:6-7: "And now you know what is restraining, that he may be revealed in his own time. For the mystery of lawlessness is already at work; only He who now restrains will do so until He is taken out of the way." The Tribulation period can't go into full force until the restraining influence in the world is taken out of the way. Who is the restrainer? There are a number of different ideas on this subject. Some believe it is human government. Some believe it is a particular law. Some believe it is some individual alive in the world.

But the Bible is very clear about what restrains in the life of an individual, and I personally believe this is a very clear reference to the Holy Spirit. The restrainer is the Holy Spirit. The Holy Spirit lives in us, and when we leave here, the Holy Spirit will leave with us. The only thing that holds this world together is the restraining influence of the Holy Spirit who lives in the hearts and lives of every single believer. The day of Tribulation cannot begin until the Holy Spirit is taken out of the way. That's going to happen when the Rapture occurs.

Discussion of the Tribulation Period

After describing the sevenfold condition of the visible Church in chapters 2 and 3, John writes about the 24 elders who are in heaven (see Revelation 4:4). He says these elders are significant because they are seated, robed, and have crowns upon their heads. These significant things suggest the 24 are symbolic representations of the Church. Where is the Church at the outset of the Tribulation period? It is seated, clothed, and crowned in heaven. The Church is not here; it is there.

Deliverance Promise

In Revelation 3, the church of Philadelphia is a prophetic picture of the true believing Church in the end days. Notice what it says in verse 10, "Because you have kept My command to persevere, I also will keep you from the hour of trial which shall come upon the whole world, to test those who dwell on the earth." This is a promise of deliverance from the time of testing.

There are some who tell us that during the Tribulation period, the Church will be here on earth; and God will miraculously keep us safe like Shadrach, Meshach, and Abed-Nego, preserved through the fire. But that is not what the Scripture says. The Bible doesn't say He will keep us from Tribulation—it says He will keep us from the very hour of the Tribulation. We will not even see the time of the Tribulation period.

Paul presents the same truth in 1 Thessalonians 5:2: "The day of the Lord so comes as a thief in the night." The coming of a thief is unexpected and unannounced. Paul uses the illustration to show that it would be foolish for him to tell them when the Tribulation would burst upon the world. He couldn't do that. It comes as a thief in the night. Then he goes on to tell them it isn't their concern anyway because "you are all sons of light and sons of the day. We are not of the night nor of darkness" (verse 5). The Tribulation is a period for those in darkness. He further affirms, "For God did not appoint us to wrath, but to obtain salvation through our Lord Jesus Christ" (verse 9). The salvation he mentions here is not the saved-from-sin salvation but a salvation or deliverance from the Tribulation period.

The Bible is so consistent. If part of God's divine program is to take His own out of judgment situations, wouldn't we also find that in the Old Testament? And we do.

Enoch was a godly man and walked with the Lord. God took him, He raptured him. The world was judged by a flood, but God took righteous Enoch out of the world.

Before Sodom and Gomorrah were judged and destroyed, Lot was taken out of Sodom. Lot asked to go to another city, and he was told by an angel, "Hurry, escape there. For I cannot do anything until you arrive there" (Genesis 19:22).

When God was going to slay the firstborn of the Egyptians, He made sure the godly people in the area were cared for with the blood on the door. They were saved before the judgment came.

Jericho was going to be destroyed. But before that happened, the spies and Rahab were taken out. The pattern of the Word of God is consistent from the beginning to the end. When judgment comes, God first of all removes His own.

Why? Because we have not been called to wrath but to salvation. Jesus paid all the penalty for our sin. The Tribulation is a time of punitive judgment from God. If we have to go through it, that says what God did through Christ on the Cross was not enough.

Doctrine of Imminency

Do you believe Jesus could come back tonight? If you do, even if you don't understand it, you are Pre-Tribulational. Because if Jesus doesn't come back for the Rapture until the seven-year Tribulation is over, then He can't come back tonight. If He doesn't come back until three and a half years into the Tribulation period, He can't come back for at least three and a half years. The only doctrine in the Bible that is proven historically from the beginning all the way through is the doctrine of the imminency of Jesus Christ. Imminency means He could come back any time. One of the reasons I believe so strongly in the Pre-Tribulational view is that it is the only view consistent with the imminent return of

Jesus Christ. The Bible teaches that the Christian waits in hope for the return of Christ. We are to be watching constantly for His return—He could come tonight.

Are you ready? You can't wait until Jesus comes back to make your decision. The Bible says in 2 Thessalonians 2:11-12 that people who have had a chance to hear the Gospel during this age of grace will not have a legitimate chance for salvation after the Rapture. It says those who have heard the Truth will be sent a strong delusion that they do not believe the Truth because they had opportunity to accept the Gospel of Christ and they rejected it. There will be people saved in the Tribulation period, but I don't believe there will be anyone saved who has heard the Gospel in this age. You won't have a second chance. You've got one chance, and it's now. Either you get ready, or you get left.

PERSONAL QUESTIONS

1. Read 2 Thessalonians 2:1-12.

   a. What are the two reasons for the Tribulation?

   b. What will happen within the Church before the Tribulation? (verse 3)

   c. What is another name for the Antichrist found in this passage? (verse 3)

d. Who is the restrainer mentioned in verses 6-7? How will the removal of the restrainer from the world impact the condition of the world?

e. How does the removal of the restrainer point to a Pre-Tribulational view of the Rapture?

f. Describe the coming of the lawless one in verses 9-10.

g. What will God send to those who didn't believe the Truth before the Rapture? (verse 11)

2. As a Christian, what peace is found in knowing you won't live through the Tribulation?

3. How does knowing those who have heard and don't respond to the Gospel before the Tribulation will not have a second chance to accept Christ impact your prayers for and conversations with others? (verses 11-12)

GROUP QUESTIONS

1. Discuss the four different views of the Tribulation mentioned at the beginning of the lesson.

   a. What is the Post-Tribulational view of the Rapture?

   b. Define the Mid-Tribulational view of the Rapture.

c. What is the partial rapture theory?

d. Define the Pre-Tribulational view of the Rapture.

e. How does the imminent return of Christ point to a Pre-Tribulational view?

f. In what way does the chapter content and overall structure of Revelation point to a Pre-Tribulational view?

2. What are some Old Testament examples that show God removing His people from judgment?

   a. What can we learn from Scripture about these examples?

   b. How do these examples point to a Pre-Tribulational view?

3. Share the peace you find in knowing you won't be on earth during the Tribulation.

4. Share how the imminence of Christ's return compels you to share the Gospel with others.

DID YOU KNOW?

Within the Body of Christ there is more than one view of the timing of the Rapture of the Church. Those holding to a *Pre-Tribulational* view believe the Rapture will occur before the beginning of the Tribulation. *Mid-Tribulationists* believe the Church will go through the first half of the Tribulation. And *Post-Tribulationists* believe the Church will be raptured after enduring the seven years of tribulation on earth. But the preponderance of biblical evidence supports the Pre-Tribulational view. Revelation 3:10 is most clear: "I also will keep you from the hour of trial which shall come upon the whole world, to test those who dwell on the earth."

THE OLIVET DISCOURSE DISCUSSION

Selected Scriptures

In this lesson we survey Jesus' teaching concerning events preceding the establishment of His kingdom on earth.

OUTLINE

Certain things in life are predictable with a measure of accuracy based on prior occurrences of the event(s). But the rule of the kingdom of God on earth, under the reign of God's Son, has never happened before. Therefore Jesus gives signs of its coming.

I. **The Passage Is Jewish**

II. **The Passage Is a Response to Questions**

III. **The Passage Is About Events to Come Before the Kingdom**
   A. The General Signs
   B. The Specific Signs

IV. **The Post-Tribulation Position**
   A. Matthew 24:31
   B. Matthew 24:40-42

V. **The Parable for Interpretation**

IN PREPARATION FOR THIS LESSON, BE SURE TO READ CHAPTER FIVE IN THE BOOK, ***The Handwriting on the Wall.***

OVERVIEW

The Rapture for all intents and purposes is rendered inconsequential if it is Post-Tribulational. If the Lord Jesus is coming again immediately at the end of the Tribulation, why do the saints need to be raptured anyway? And if all believers are raptured and glorified just prior to the inauguration of the kingdom age, then there will be no one to populate and propagate the kingdom. They will all be gone. Post-Tribulationists teach a kind of yo-yo principle of the Rapture. They tell us at the end of the Tribulation we will go up and then come right back down. But there is no purpose for that and no reason for it from the Scripture.

The character of God as a God of grace demands that the Church escape the Tribulation period because the majority of them have already escaped by dying. What good purpose could God have for a small group who just happen to be left at the end of time to be subjected to the Tribulation?

Another problem with the Post-Tribulation view is that there needs to be a period of time between the Rapture and the Second Advent of Jesus Christ in order for certain things to take place that are programmed in Scripture. The Bible teaches that during the Tribulation, the Judgment Seat of Christ will take place in heaven. Believers will be brought before the Bema Seat to give an answer for the things done in the body. The Marriage Supper of the Lamb will also convene during that time.

God's program is this: When the Church age is over, Christ will come, and His own will be caught up to meet Him. The dead in Christ shall rise first, then those who are alive shall be caught up to be with the Lord. Immediately after that, the Tribulation period begins on earth; the Judgment Seat of Christ begins in heaven. For seven years the judgment of God against unbelieving Israel and Gentile rebels will take place on earth. At the end of that time, Christ will come back in His Second Coming, the Second Advent.

The difference between the Rapture and the Second Advent is that in the Rapture, Christ comes for His saints. In the Second Advent, Christ comes with His saints to reign on earth. If you don't distinguish between the two, you will always be confused about prophecy.

THE PASSAGE IS JEWISH

Matthew 24 and 25, commonly referred to as the Olivet Discourse, is a passage of Scripture that deals with the Tribulation period. It has particular reference to the Jews. The sections of Matthew 24, Mark 13, Luke 17, and Luke 21 ought to be studied together. In these passages of Scripture, Jesus speaks to the Jewish people about preparation for Christ's return and the nature of the kingdom. These passages deal with questions the disciples asked. The disciples here are not representatives of the Church. They are representatives of Israel. In Matthew 24, the Church was not in the minds of the disciples. They didn't know about the Church or the Rapture yet.

Matthew 24 and 25 is a Jewish passage of Scripture. First of all, it takes place in Judea. Matthew 24:20 references a Jewish celebration, the Sabbath. Matthew 24:15 references the abomination prophesied by Daniel concerning the Jews. This concerns what will happen in the middle of the Tribulation when the temple is desecrated. We often use the word "elect" to refer to the Church. But in this passage it is a reference to the Jews—those who are selected by God in a special way.

Luke 21 is dealing with God's message and place for the nation of Israel as He communicates it with the representatives of the Jews, the disciples. The Church is not mentioned. The Rapture is not mentioned. There is no clear evidence that they are even in the minds of anybody in that discussion.

THE PASSAGE IS A RESPONSE TO QUESTIONS

The Olivet Discourse was delivered by Christ during the last week before the Crucifixion. In essence, it was a response to some questions that were asked Him by the disciples. The first question was, "When will the temple be destroyed?" The second question was, "What will be the sign of Your coming?" The third question was, "What will be the sign of the end of the age?" (Matthew 24:3)

> **"JESUS SAID HE would return and He will. In the meantime, it serves no good purpose to stand around staring at the sky. There's work to do! Our faith assures us that He will return, but our *focus* must be on accomplishing the King's business until that great day arrives."**
>
> DR. DAVID JEREMIAH, *Jesus' Final Warning*

Christ answered the first question in another passage of Scripture. The prophecy was fulfilled in A.D. 70 when Jerusalem was destroyed and the temple was flattened.

The last two questions have to do with the End Times. It was not appropriate for Jesus Christ to speak directly of the Rapture at this time because the disciples were not prepared to understand it. Jesus had not instructed them about the Church yet, and it was not until the apostle Paul that the full-blown truth of the Church was brought into existence. The Church was a mystery to them—"a truth that has been known from the beginning of time but has not yet been revealed," according to the New Testament meaning of "mystery." They could not understand the Rapture if they did not understand the Church, so there is no reason to expect it in this passage.

The disciples' first question indicates they were primarily concerned with when the temple was going to be destroyed. The temple was the most magnificent thing in the world in their day. If the temple were to be destroyed, the world would be over as far as the Jews were concerned.

The end of the temple would be synonymous with the End Times, so their next questions were logical. "Lord, when the temple is destroyed, then Your Second Coming must be shortly after that, and what is the sign? How shall we know when the End Time comes?"

The coming of Christ and the end of the age are the same. But it is questionable if the disciples clearly understood at that time that there would be a period of time between the first coming and the second coming of Christ. The disciples were asking, "Lord, when are You going to come and establish Your kingdom? We thought You were going to do it now, but You haven't done it. So when can we expect You to come back and do what we thought You were going to do when You were here the first time?"

The Passage Is About Events to Come Before the Kingdom

The whole issue of Matthew 24 and 25 has nothing to do with the Rapture by specific reference. It has everything to do with the events that are going to come immediately before Christ comes to set up His kingdom. The events that take place immediately before the kingdom will be the Tribulation events. Since Jesus in this passage is teaching the disciples what would happen immediately before the kingdom is established, He runs through the events of the Tribulation period.

The General Signs

The first thing Jesus does in Matthew 24 is to state the general signs that lead up to the Second Coming. He talks of people pretending to be Christ, of wars and rumors of wars, of famines and pestilence and earthquakes. He runs the events in front of them in panoramic form. These are the events of the Tribulation period that immediately precede the kingdom.

The Specific Signs

The second thing Jesus does is give the specific sign of the beginning of the Great Tribulation. The Great Tribulation is halfway through the Tribulation period. The Tribulation is bad, but the Great Tribulation is worse. The events which transpire in the last three and a half years are the worst events which take place in all of the world's history.

The specific thing that will happen before the beginning of the Great Tribulation is the abomination. Jesus says, "Therefore when you see the 'abomination of desolation,' spoken of by Daniel the prophet, standing in the holy place" (Matthew 24:15), and then He goes on to describe what it will be like immediately before the kingdom. He basically tells them it will be so awful they should run for their lives without looking back.

The details of the Tribulation are expanded upon in Revelation 4-18. What Jesus is teaching in Matthew 24 is not what will happen before the Rapture. The Lord is teaching the disciples, in answer to their questions, what will happen before the kingdom is established. Some people are bothered that He doesn't mention the Rapture, but He had no reason to. He will give the disciples information about the Rapture in due time.

The Post-Tribulation Position

Matthew 24:31

The Post-Tribulationists try to place the Church in Matthew 24 by referring to verse 31, "And He will send His angels with a great sound of a trumpet, and they will gather together His elect from the four winds, from one end of heaven to the other." The Bible teaches clearly that immediately before the Millennium starts there will be a gathering of the elect in preparation for the Millennium, but that is not the Rapture. There is no mention here of the translation of any saints. There is not one word concerning a resurrection. First Thessalonians 4 tells us that associated with the Rapture is the resurrection of those who are dead in Christ. There is nothing here that has the earmark of the Rapture. It is simply a reference to the final gathering of the elect before the Millennial period begins.

Matthew 24:40-42

Another place Post-Tribulationists try to insinuate the Rapture into this chapter is in verses 40-42: "Then two men will be in the field: one will be taken and the other left. Two women will be grinding at the mill: one will be taken and the other left. Watch therefore, for you do not know what hour your Lord is coming." The Bible teaches that the Rapture will be like this. But this passage does not speak of the Rapture. A few verses earlier, the word for "taken" was used to explain how those not saved by the Flood at the time of Noah were taken. How were they taken? They were taken in judgment, not in Rapture. When the Flood came, those who had rejected Noah's message were not raptured. They were taken away by the Flood in judgment. What this passage is teaching is that in the day of the Tribulation when the Lord comes in judgment upon this earth, some will be judged like that, independently, immediately. There won't be a mass judgment totally across the whole world, but independent individuals will be judged. One will be judged, another left.

> **"I WISH I could be alive when Christ returns because I would like to be the first earthly monarch to take my crown and lay it at his feet."**
>
> QUEEN ELIZABETH I OF ENGLAND

The companion passage in Luke 17 ends with Jesus' answer to the disciples' question about where they would be taken: "Wherever the body is, there the eagles will be gathered together" (verse 37). He was talking about the vultures that are going to get their carcasses in judgment, not the Rapture.

THE PARABLE FOR INTERPRETATION

The parable that our Lord used is the key as to how we interpret this passage for today in advance of these events. He said, "Now learn this parable from the fig tree: When its branch has already become tender and puts forth leaves, you know that summer is near. So you also, when you see all these things, know that it is near—at the doors!" (Matthew 24:32-33)

We do not know the exact times and seasons, but I do believe the Bible teaches that we can know when we are nearing the time of the end of all things. Jesus was teaching His disciples a valid principle of Bible interpretation—coming events cast their shadows before them. I don't mean to suggest there are signs that need to be fulfilled before the Rapture can take place, but the Lord does say that if you study Scripture and look at God's movements and the affairs of humanity, you will have some indication of when God is setting the stage that will consummate in the Second Coming of the Son of God.

One of the signs Jesus said would come to pass before the kingdom was set up is famines. There are famines today all over this globe. I personally believe the next great crisis will be universal famine. All you have to do is ponder the population explosion.

It is not wrong to say the signs are telling us the Lord's coming draws nigh. It is wrong to say that all of these things happen and then the Rapture comes. That's not what this passage is teaching.

What prophecy does for us more than anything else is give us a perspective on the future, a certain knowledge that Christ is in control. He has a plan and a program. He might come today; but if He doesn't, I am going to live my life to the fullest, accomplishing what He has given me to do. Jesus is coming again.

PERSONAL QUESTIONS

1. Read Matthew 24.
   a. Who is the audience for the Olivet Discourse? What words within the Olivet Discourse make the audience clear to us? (verses 3, 15, 20)

   b. What questions did the disciples ask Jesus? (verses 1-3)

   c. Why were these logical questions for them to ask?

   d. Why were the disciples primarily concerned with the destruction of the temple?

   e. What events are described in the Olivet Discourse?

f. When will these events take place?

g. Why didn't Jesus speak directly about the Rapture?

h. What are the general signs the kingdom is coming? The specific signs?

i. Explain the difference between the Tribulation and the Great Tribulation.

2. How should you live in light of the Second Coming of Christ? What changes might you need to make to accomplish what God has given you to do during your time on earth?

GROUP QUESTIONS

1. Turn to Matthew 24 together.

   a. What is the order of events for God's program for the End Times?

   b. What is the difference between the Rapture and the Second Coming?

   c. What instructions does Jesus give for those on earth after they see "the abomination of desolation" take place? (verses 15-20)

   d. How does the parable of the fig tree help us interpret the signs of today in advance of these events? (verses 32-33)

2. Discuss verses 40-42. What will happen to the individuals who are taken?

   a. What points to these verses not referring to the Rapture?

   b. How will those who are taken be judged?

3. Share how understanding prophecy impacts how you live your life. If applicable, share what changes you are going to make in your life in order to accomplish the tasks God has given you during your time here on earth.

DID YOU KNOW?

Matthew 24:34 is one of the most difficult verses in the four Gospels: "This generation will by no means pass away till all these things take place." Did Jesus mean the generation to whom He was speaking? Or should *genea* (generation) be rendered in its rare use of "race," referring to the Jewish race not passing away? Or was Jesus referring to the generation that witnessed the events of which He was speaking just before He made the statement in verse 34—the generation that begins to witness the signs of His appearing (verse 30)? Given the context, this last interpretation seems most reasonable. Once the events of the End Times begin to happen, they will unfold quickly—within one generation.

SUPERPOWERS IN CONFLICT

Daniel 8:1-8, 15-21

In this lesson we learn the contents and meaning of Daniel's second vision.

OUTLINE

A principle in the early days of Israel's history said that if a prophet's words didn't come true, he was a false prophet. Daniel's prophetic words came true in a shocking degree of detail. His vision of the Medes, Persians, and Greeks was fulfilled exactly as he saw it.

I. The Reception of Daniel's Second Vision

A. The Position of the Vision
B. The Profile of the Vision
C. The Place of the Vision
D. The Purpose of the Vision
E. The Paraphrase of the Vision
F. The Plan of the Vision

II. The Revelation of Daniel's Second Vision

A. The Ram
B. The Goat

III. The Resolution of Daniel's Second Vision

A. A Great Prophecy
B. A Great Principle
C. A Great Person

IN PREPARATION FOR THIS LESSON, BE SURE TO READ CHAPTER THIRTEEN IN THE BOOK, ***The Handwriting on the Wall.***

OVERVIEW

Quite often when I talk to people who are not students of the Bible, they focus on the strange nature of biblical information. They say things like, "The Bible is really a weird book. Take Daniel—there are animals everywhere. You read the Book of Revelation, there are all kinds of weird symbols and signs and animals. How in the world is anybody supposed to understand anything when they're trying to tell great truth by using animals? I mean, nobody ever uses animals in communication."

But the fact is, we do. Sometimes we look back on the times when the Scripture was being written and think: They just communicated in a different way than we do today. But is it really that different? What about these statements?

My grandfather is as wise as an owl.
He eats like a horse.
I know I should stand up to her, but I guess I'm just chicken.
She has the memory of an elephant.
Sometimes he's as dumb as an ox.
My husband is as stubborn as a mule.

Isn't it interesting to realize communication hasn't changed all that much? As we study the eighth chapter of Daniel, we will discover that the animals in this story are unique because they have a special meaning in the time in which this prophecy was written.

THE RECEPTION OF DANIEL'S SECOND VISION

The Position of the Vision

Daniel 8 records the second vision that Daniel personally received. Let me remind you that the book is put together in two sections. Chapters 1 through 6 are history. Chapters 7–12 are prophecies that were received during the time of the first six chapters. Daniel's vision in chapter 8 actually took place chronologically between the fourth and fifth chapters. That is important to understand because what God communicates to Daniel in the eighth chapter prepares him to understand what he needs to know when he walks on the scene in the fifth chapter. This vision came to Daniel just before the tragic events of the end of the Babylonian Empire. What Daniel saw in the vision helped him to know how to decipher the handwriting on the wall.

This second vision came to Daniel in about 550 or 549 B.C. At that point in time, Daniel was about sixty to sixty-seven years old. Two years elapsed between the vision he had in chapter 7 and the vision in chapter 8.

The Profile of the Vision

In Daniel 2, God gave Daniel the whole panorama of Gentile history from the time of Babylon to the End Times, even to the divided Roman Empire in the future. He communicated this as a gigantic image. In chapter 8, God zooms in on the middle section of that image. We will see just the arms, shoulders, and torso. Chapter 8 isn't about Babylon or Rome. It's about the Persians and the Medes and the Greeks.

The entire focus from now on in Daniel is on the Gentile powers only as they relate to the Jews. It was under the Persian government that the Jews were allowed to return from Babylon and set up their land and worship again. It was under the Romans that the temple and the city were ultimately destroyed.

In the original language of the Old Testament, there is a change of language in chapter 8. In chapters 2–7, the language is Aramaic, the Gentile language of the day. In the eighth chapter, Hebrew is used once again because the coming events foretold will affect the Jews.

In Daniel 8:9, there is a name that gives a clue to the significance of the Israelites in this prophecy. "And out of one of them came a little horn which grew exceedingly great toward the south, toward the east, and toward the Glorious Land." The Glorious Land is Israel.

The Place of the Vision

When the prophecy came to Daniel, he was transported in his vision to Shushan, the city of the palace. At that particular time, Shushan was a little, insignificant city in the fringe area of the Babylonian kingdom—an unknown place with absolutely no significance to the Babylonian kingdom.

> **"THE LAND OF Israel has been the nerve center of the world since the time of Abraham. When Jesus Christ came to earth, Israel became the truth center of the world. There is coming a day in the future (the Millennium) when the land will be the peace center of the world. Today, as we look at that small piece of real estate in the Middle East, it is the storm center of the world."**
>
> DR. DAVID JEREMIAH, *The Handwriting on the Wall–Secrets from the Prophecies of Daniel*

Later on it became the very nerve center of the next kingdom. Daniel is in the very center of that prophecy in his mind's eye.

The Purpose of the Vision

The purpose of this vision was to prepare Daniel for the end of the Babylonian kingdom and help him know what to say and do when he walked into the drunken party and saw the handwriting on the wall. It helped him understand that God was saying to Belshazzar that the Babylonian kingdom was over. The Medes and Persians were on their way. It was doomsday for Babylon. The next dynasty was about to begin.

Daniel was told that the vision was about the time of the end. God was not just talking about the end of that particular time. He was positioning Himself to tell Daniel about the end of time itself, when the kingdoms of this world will be assimilated into the kingdom of our God.

The Paraphrase of the Vision

Daniel was emotionally involved in the vision God gave him. In fact, he became so emotional that he fainted and was sick for several days. He didn't know what the vision meant, so God sent someone to tell him. He didn't send just anybody; He sent Gabriel. When God had something special to share, He dispatched Gabriel.

The Plan of the Vision

God didn't send unorganized visions to His prophets. He always planned them so the prophets would understand exactly what was going on. In essence, God was teaching Daniel what is ultimately the truth concerning the man whom we know as the Antichrist. But in order for God to get the message through to Daniel, He gave it to him in a threefold measure. He looks out into the future with a king "having fierce features" (Daniel 8:23). That is the Antichrist. Then He gives Daniel two earlier persons in history who are pictures of the Antichrist. Each of these three personages is labeled as a horn: the big horn, the little horn and the final horn. In Daniel, the word "horn" stands for king or power or kingdom. These three horns are three kings.

The Revelation of Daniel's Second Vision

The Ram

The first animal Daniel saw was a ram with two horns. The horns are explained in verse 20 as the kings of Media and Persia. The ram is the Medo-Persian Empire. The prophecy meticulously describes one of the horns as being higher than the other, and the higher one came up last. This shows how the Medes came first and were joined by the Persians. The Persian Empire assimilated the Median Empire just as the prophecy showed.

The Goat

The first colony of Greece was established by an oracle that sent a goat for a guide to build a city in an unknown place. The goat came to the region of Greece. In gratitude for the goat leading them in the right direction, the city was built and called "aegae," meaning goat. The goat was Greece.

In Daniel 8:5-7 are five of the most amazing prophecies I have ever studied, amazingly fulfilled down to the minutest detail. The first prophecy has to do with the route to world conquest of the Greeks. It says when the goat began to move out of the west and cover the whole earth, it moved so rapidly that it didn't touch the ground. When the Greek Empire began to grow, conquests amassed so quickly that Greece set world records for bringing the world under its dominion. In twelve brief years, the Greeks conquered the entire civilized world, never losing a battle. God said that was how it would happen before it ever took place.

The second amazing prophecy has to do with the reputation of the king. The Scripture says that the horn in the middle of the forehead of the goat was the first king of Greece (see verse 21). Who was the first king of Greece? Alexander the Great. Alexander was the son of Philip of Macedon and Olympias. When Alexander was growing

> "Tradition says that when Alexander was on his way to conquer Jerusalem, a Jewish priest gave him a copy of the Book of Daniel and said, 'You must read this; you are in this book!' Alexander read the prophecy about himself and got down on his knees and worshiped God."
>
> Dr. David Jeremiah, *The Handwriting on the Wall–Secrets from the Prophecies of Daniel*

up, his mother taught him he was a descendant of Achilles and Hercules. His father was a great militarist and leader. Yet he told his son, "Alexander, my son, seek out a kingdom worthy of yourself. Macedonia is too small for you." Alexander went for the world and got it. I wonder how much of that was built into him because of the faith his parents had in him.

The third prophecy has to do with the ruin of the Medo-Persian Empire. God told Daniel when the notable horn, the great king, came to power, he would go against the Persians and the Medes. When Alexander finally decided to take the Medes and Persians down, he came with 35,000 troops from the west, defeated the Persian army under Darius III, and freed all of the Greek cities of Asia Minor from the Persians. He refused to negotiate with Darius, swept on south, took Egypt, Tyre, Gaza, then retraced his steps through Syria and met an enlarged Persian army. This time he wiped out the Medo-Persian Empire just like God said he would, two hundred years before it happened.

The fourth amazing prophecy has to do with the remarkable death of the king. When Alexander conquered the Medo-Persians, he sacked several other Persian cities and swept on to India; but his tired army had had enough, and they returned to Babylon where Alexander died at the age of 33. He was a victim of his own drunkenness and fever, depressed in his own spirit because there weren't any more worlds for him to conquer. When he was strong at the height of his glory, the great horn was broken (see verse 8).

The last great prophecy of this chapter has to do with the reorganization of the Greek Empire. The prophecy said that when Alexander died, his kingdom would be divided in four, given to four kings who were not as strong as Alexander, and the power of the total kingdom would be dissipated. For twenty years after Alexander's death all kinds of struggling and infighting persisted. Within that period of time the kingdom of Alexander was divided between four of his generals. All of this was written long before it ever happened.

The Resolution of Daniel's Second Vision

A Great Prophecy

This is a great prophecy. Here is prophecy written down about things we now know took place exactly as God said they would. The Antichrist hasn't come yet, but he will. When you study prophecy, you see how literally it is fulfilled.

A Great Principle

Here is a great principle. Daniel's reaction to the prophecy was emotional, even physical. We usually respond to God's Word by taking it for granted. I believe God would have us get serious about His Book as Daniel did. When we read about the coming Antichrist who is going to devastate those who have been left behind, we should begin to look around for those who don't know Jesus Christ and ask God to help us get them in the kingdom before His prophecy comes true.

A Great Person

This prophecy introduces a great man. Alexander was a powerful man, a great dictator and ruler, a great general and leader. It's easy to compare him to another great One who died at 33. By all of the standards of humanism and world history, Alexander stands rank and file above our Lord. But there's not a person who has ever walked with Jesus for one day who would debate the issue for a moment. Jesus is the greatest!

PERSONAL QUESTIONS

1. Read Daniel 8:1-8, 15-21.
   a. When did this vision occur during Daniel's life?

   b. How did this vision prepare Daniel for the end of the Babylonian kingdom?

   c. Where was Daniel transported to in his vision? (verse 2)

   d. Whom does God send to explain the vision to Daniel? (verses 16-17)

e. What kingdom did the ram represent? (verse 20)

f. What kingdom did the goat represent? (verse 21)

g. Whom did the "large horn" represent? (verse 21)

h. Whom did the four horns represent? (verse 8)

2. Read Daniel 8:27.

   a. What happens to Daniel after he has the vision?

   b. How do you think you would react if you were in Daniel's place?

   c. Does God's Word impact you the way it impacted Daniel?

   d. What can you do this week to dig deeper into God's Word?

GROUP QUESTIONS

1. Turn to Daniel 8:1-8, 15-21 together.

   a. Where does this vision fit chronologically in the book of Daniel?

   b. How does the change of language from Aramaic in chapters 2–7 to Hebrew in chapter 8 help us understand who these events will affect?

   c. What animals does Daniel see in his vision? (verses 3-8)

d. What interaction occurs between the two animals? (verses 6-7)

e. Discuss how Alexander the Great and the Greek Empire fulfilled the prophecy given in verses 5-8.

f. How quickly and decisively did Greece conquer the surrounding nations? (verse 5)

g. How did Alexander conquer the Medo-Persian Empire?

2. Discuss God's plan for this vision. What was God teaching Daniel through the vision?

3. Turn to Daniel 8:27 together.

   a. How did the vision impact Daniel physically?

   b. What does Daniel's reaction teach us about the importance of God's Word?

   c. Share how Daniel's reaction challenges you to dig deeper into God's Word.

DID YOU KNOW?

The nation-conquering exploits of Alexander the Great resulted in what is now referred to as the Hellenistic period in world history, when Greek culture reigned from Italy in the west and beyond Mesopotamia to the borders of modern China and India in the east and Egypt in the south. The Hellenistic period is usually dated from the death of Alexander in Babylon in 323 B.C. to around 150 B.C. when Rome gained sway over the heart of the Greek Empire. Important for biblical history, Israel was ruled by Greeks until Roman dominance replaced it. The New Testament was written in the Greek language, and the most-used version of the Old Testament was the Septuagint, a Greek translation prepared by Jewish scholars in Egypt.

ANTIOCHUS AND THE ANTICHRIST

Daniel 8:9-14, 22-27

In this lesson we meet a historical figure who was a type of the Antichrist.

OUTLINE

In the Old Testament, many people, places, and events prefigured people, places, and events appearing in the New Testament. Even evil was prefigured. Antiochus Epiphanes was a Hellenistic ruler who persecuted the Jews—a type of the Antichrist to come.

I. Antiochus Epiphanes

II. Antichrist—Characteristics

A. Dramatic in Appearance
B. Destined to Do Evil
C. Dynamic Leadership
D. Demonic in Power
E. Destructive in His Reign
F. Deceitful in His Practice
G. Deifies Himself
H. Disguises His Cruelty With Peace Promises
I. Destroyed Without Human Hand

IN PREPARATION FOR THIS LESSON, BE SURE TO READ CHAPTER THIRTEEN IN THE BOOK, ***The Handwriting on the Wall.***

OVERVIEW

When Daniel speaks of the Antichrist who is coming and the antichrists who have come, that is not an empty prophecy. It is a truth validated by the mail I receive. Parts of one letter written to me said, "I am the one God has sent to be the return of Christ. Ask the F.B.I. I have proven it to them as well as to many others. . . . We are a team, God, Jesus, and myself. We are the Holy Trinity whether you believe it or not, and if you don't, to hell with you! We don't need you, you need us. . . . If you have any intentions of getting to heaven it must be through me, for I am here now and doing God's will, and I have that say so, and I say that you shall never go to heaven unless and until you recognize me. I am the second Christ. Make no mistake about that."

This guy is serious. He has come to the conclusion that in his lifetime he is the one Christ has sent. He believes he is Jesus Christ. The Bible says there are many coming who will say they are Christ. Daniel's prophecy in the eighth chapter is to the effect that there is an Antichrist coming.

Antiochus Epiphanes

Daniel 8 is built around three people: two people of historical significance and one prophetic individual. The notable or great horn was Alexander the Great. He illustrates the power of the coming Antichrist. He is followed in the text by the little horn. He came out of one of the kingdoms ruled over by one of Alexander's generals. We know now that was Seleucus' kingdom. Scripture records him as "a little horn which grew exceedingly great" (verse 9). The prophecy is fulfilled in a person in history known as Antiochus Epiphanes. His name means "Antiochus God Manifest" or "Antiochus the great one of God."

According to history, he persecuted people. In Egypt, when he was on his way to conquer the world, he was stopped by the armies of Rome. In fury and frustration, Antiochus turned his forces away from Egypt and marched up through the maritime border of the Mediterranean. He vented his anger by taking his army to Jerusalem and sacking the city. During that march, Antiochus killed 80,000 Jews. He took 40,000 of the people and sold them into slavery. He also plundered the temple. He took the golden altar of incense and stood before the inner veil. He decided to destroy the Jewish religion and substitute for it Greek worship and Greek culture.

Instead of the Feast of the Tabernacles, Antiochus Epiphanes celebrated in the temple the feast of Bacchanalia, worshiping Bacchus, the god of pleasure and wine. He forced the Jews to observe the Saturnalia, worshiping Saturn, using harlots in the temple for those feast days. He forbade the observance of the Sabbath. He not only forbade the reading of the Scriptures, but he also burned every copy of the Torah he could find. Any Jewish practice was forbidden on penalty of death. He did everything he could to desecrate and destroy their religion forever.

Antiochus forced the Jews to observe all of his feast days and forbade the institution of circumcision. History records in the Book of Maccabees that there were two mothers, deeply committed to their Jewish culture, who determined to circumcise their boys. When Antiochus heard about it, he took the babies and killed them, hung them around each mother's neck, marched the women through the city streets of Jerusalem up to the highest wall and flung them, babies and all, headlong over the wall.[1]

> "[ANTIOCHUS EPIPHANES] FARMED **out the [Jewish] high priesthood to the highest bidder and employed it as a collection agency for the government. Menelaus succeeded in outbidding Jason to the extent of three hundred talents and gained the high priesthood!"**
>
> WILLIAM HENDRIKSEN, *Survey of the Bible*

One mother who had seven sons defied Antiochus' law. Antiochus cut the tongues out of the boys' mouths and then fried the boys to death, one at a time, on a flatiron. Then he murdered the mother. This is just a short vignette of a long history of agony under Antiochus Epiphanes. He tried to strip every semblance of the Jewish faith from the Jews.

When the Scripture speaks of the desecration of the temple (see Daniel 8:13), it is speaking of the time Antiochus walked into the sacred place of the Jews with a sow. He slit the throat of the sow and sacrificed the pig on the altar of the Jewish people. Then he took the juice from that animal and sprayed it all over the inside of the temple. Everything that was holy to the Jews had sow's blood all over it.

In a vision, Daniel heard a holy one ask another holy one how long it would go on. The reply was 2,300 days, or literally, evenings and mornings. Scholars differ in their understanding of that terminology. If we take the 2,300 evenings/mornings to represent morning sacrifice and evening sacrifice, we get 1,250 days. That fits, although not exactly, into the three and a half years of the first half of the Tribulation. If we take the 2,300 as full days, that fits the seven-year period, but not exactly.

The atrocities of Antiochus did end. There was living in those days a priest in a place called Modein, just outside of Jerusalem. The priest's name was Mattathias. He was a patriarch and grieved over the sorrow of his people. One day an emissary from Antiochus came to Modein to make the Jews bow down before the altar of Jupiter, the Greek god. When a Jew came to worship Jupiter, Mattathias killed him, then he killed the officer that made the Jew bow down. And the Maccabean revolt was on. Mattathias was old and died before the revolt was over. He passed his torch on to his third son, Judas Maccabaeus, who won the victory over Antiochus and independence for the Jews.

When Judas Maccabaeus went back in to cleanse the temple, he wanted to light the lamps in the temple. The ceremony to reconsecrate the temple required eight days, but he only found enough oil for one day. Tradition says the one cruse of oil lasted not only for the first day, but it also lasted throughout all eight days. In celebration of that miraculous reconsecration of the temple, the Jewish people celebrate Hanukkah.

Antichrist—Characteristics

As the leadership of Alexander demonstrates the power of the coming Antichrist, Antiochus Epiphanes demonstrates the cruelty of the coming Antichrist. In Daniel 8:23 we see the final person, the one toward whom all of this prophetic information is pointing. God prophesied concerning Alexander and Antiochus, and history validates the prophecy. These were real people. Just as those two men of history came to pass, the prophecy concerning the Antichrist will literally come to pass. The stage is being set even now. The interesting thing is that the characteristics of these other two men merge together in what we learn about the king with fierce features, the Antichrist.

Dramatic in Appearance

When the Antichrist comes at the end of time, he will be dramatic in appearance. In the latter time of their kingdom, when the climactic time has come, when everything has happened that points to the advance of evil, the king of fierce countenance will make his appearance. Every prophetic truth in the Old and New Testaments has some relationship to the coming of the Antichrist.

Destined to Do Evil

The Scripture says that the Antichrist will come "when the transgressors have reached their fullness" (verse 23). When evil is at its worst, when things are happening you can't even imagine happening, when all the restraints are lifted and everything seems to be going full-blown in the direction of evil and Satan, at that moment the Antichrist will walk across the scene.

Dynamic Leadership

Verse 23 says the king will arise who understands "dark sentences" (KJV). This refers both to his ability to solve problems and to his dynamic leadership. He will be a man who will walk into the frame of reference of our world and have all the right answers. Some expositors believe this matter of "dark sentences" is a reference to the fact that he will be involved with the occult.

Demonic in Power

Verse 24 says, "His power shall be mighty, but not by his own power." That means he will be demonic, demon-possessed. Revelation 13:2 says the Dragon gave to the Antichrist his power and his seat and his great authority. In the future, when the Antichrist walks on this earth, he will be indwelt by Satan. I can't help but believe that Antiochus Epiphanes must have been Satan-filled in order to commit the atrocities he did. He was demonic just as the Antichrist will be.

Destructive in His Reign

"He shall destroy fearfully" (Daniel 8:24). The whole world will wonder at his destructiveness. And he will "prosper and thrive; he shall destroy the mighty, and also the holy people." Antiochus did this. Alexander did this. And the Antichrist will do it. In the prophecies concerning the Tribulation period, there are times when blood is let to such a degree it is up to the level of the bridles of the horses. The stench of fallen flesh will be so great that when the ships pass the harbor from the place where the battles are fought, those sailing will have to stop their noses because of the overwhelming odor. Everything I know about Antiochus Epiphanes causes me to shudder, but when I think the Antichrist will be that man multiplied a hundred times over, I cannot imagine the evil that will run rampant on this earth during that seven-year period.

> "I BELIEVE GOD wants us to get serious about this Book. When we read about the coming Man of Sin, the one who is going to rule this world and destroy those who have been left behind, it should compel us to look at those around us and tell them about the accurate prophecies in God's Word. The prophetic Word of God ought to motivate us to see our planet as a world that is lost."
>
> DR. DAVID JEREMIAH, *The Handwriting on the Wall–Secrets from the Prophecies of Daniel*

Deceitful in His Practice

"Through his cunning he shall cause deceit to prosper under his rule" (verse 25). The Antichrist will come telling everyone he is God and doing lying wonders. The Antichrist will be the great deceiver. He will come with lies and wonders and deceive the people, just as Antiochus did.

Deifies Himself

On the coins printed during Antiochus' reign were the words, "Theos Antiochus Theos Epiphanes." That means, "Antiochus the Great, God Manifest." He said he was God, just like the Antichrist will when he comes. He will deify himself.

Disguises His Cruelty With Peace Promises

"And by peace [he] shall destroy many" (verse 25, KJV). There is coming a day when the Antichrist, in order to make peace with the Jews, will make a covenant with them at the beginning of the Tribulation period. He'll promise them they can worship and observe their feast days. He'll gain their confidence by deceit and then break the covenant. All hell will break out. That will usher in the Great Tribulation, the time of great suffering on this earth.

Antiochus Epiphanes foreshadowed this quality in the coming Antichrist. Historical sources describe how he perfectly pictured this quality: "And after two years fully expired the king sent his chief collector of tribute unto the cities of Judah, who came unto Jerusalem with a great multitude, and spake peacable words unto them, but all was deceit: for when they had given him credence, he fell suddenly upon the city, and smote it very sore, and destroyed much people of Israel."[2] Promises of peace followed by destruction.

Destroyed Without Human Hand

The Antichrist will be "broken without human means" (Daniel 8:25). He will be supernaturally killed. Even in this Antiochus Epiphanes illustrates the Antichrist. He made great strides in his godless purge until finally, because the Jews had cast the image of Jupiter out of the temple, he became embittered and claimed he would make Jerusalem a common burial place. No sooner had Antiochus made this declaration that he was afflicted with an incurable disease. His sufferings were unbearable, and the stench from his own body was so horrible even Antiochus couldn't stand the smell. Finding it impossible to fulfill his threat, he frankly confessed that he knew he was suffering because of what he had done to the Jews and their worship. He died in misery, a foolish man who thought he could resist God and get away with it. He was brought down supernaturally without a human hand touching him.

How does that apply to the Antichrist? He will not end naturally, either. One day King Jesus will ride out of glory and go into combat with that old boy. The end of it will be that the Antichrist will be cast into hell.

Notes

1. 1 Maccabees 1:29-30.
2. Ibid.

PERSONAL QUESTIONS

1. Read Daniel 8:9-14, 22-27.

   a. To whom does "their kingdom" refer? (verse 23)

   b. What do "fierce features" and "sinister schemes" suggest about his character and intent? (verse 23)

   c. What does "not by his own power" suggest about who is behind his activity? (verse 24)

d. Why does his attempt to destroy "the holy people" cast him as a type of Antichrist to come? (verse 24)

e. How successful is he at first in ruling over the Jews in Israel? (verse 24)

f. What does self-exaltation say about his motives and his motivation? (verse 25)

g. Who was Antiochus' ultimate enemy? (verse 25)

2. Describe the evil Antiochus did during his reign.

   a. How did he treat the Jewish people?

   b. What are some religious practices Antiochus forbid the Jews from practicing?

c. What feasts did he require the Jews to observe?

d. How did his laws impact the Jews ability to practice their religion?

e. How did Antiochus desecrate the temple?

3. Have you been moved to pray more urgently for those who don't know Christ as Savior after studying about the Antichrist? If so, what changes will you make to your prayer life to reflect this?

GROUP QUESTIONS

1. Turn to Daniel 8:9-14, 22-27 together.

   a. What three people is Daniel 8 built around?

   b. What characteristics of the coming Antichrist did Alexander the Great and Antiochus Epiphanes demonstrate?

   c. How many days will the desecration of the temple last? (verse 14)

   d. What are the two ways scholars interpret these days?

2. Discuss how this passage not only points to Antiochus Epiphanes and Alexander but also to the Antichrist.

   a. How do the characteristics of Antiochus and Alexander merge together in foreshadowing the Antichrist?

   b. Who will be behind the Antichrist's power? (verse 24)

   c. What does the phrase "understands sinister schemes" in verse 25 tell us about the Antichrist's leadership?

d. How did Antiochus foreshadow how the Antichrist will disguise cruelty with peaceful promises?

e. Share how learning more about the Antichrist compels you to prayer and evangelism.

DID YOU KNOW?

Hanukkah, celebrated annually by observant Jews, has its roots in the time of Antiochus Epiphanes (164 B.C.). Antiochus persecuted the Jews terribly and desecrated the temple in Jerusalem. A Jewish priest named Mattathias decided to resist Antiochus. A full-fledged rebellion ensued, known as the Maccabean revolt after the name of Mattathias' family. When Mattathias died, his son Judas assumed leadership of the revolt. The cleansing of the temple required eight days, but there was only enough oil for the lamps for one day. That one day's worth of oil supposedly lasted for eight days. The miracle that allowed the restoration of the temple is celebrated today as Hanukkah ("consecration").

God's Word and Prayer

Daniel 9:1-4

In this lesson we discover what motivated Daniel to be a man of prayer.

OUTLINE

Daniel was one of the most imitable characters in the Old Testament. He was steadfast in his faith, loyal to his God, respectful yet firm in his convictions, and a dynamic leader. Not the least of his qualities was his commitment to the importance of prayer.

I. Life-Changing Prayer Is Motivated by the Word of God

II. Life-Changing Prayer Is Measured by the Will of God

III. Life-Changing Prayer Is Manifested in Our Walk With God

A. Frequency of Prayer

B. Fervency of Prayer

In preparation for this lesson, be sure to read chapter fourteen in the book, ***The Handwriting on the Wall.***

OVERVIEW

Leonard Ravenhill has written of the Church, "We have many organizers, but few agonizers; many players and payers, but few pray-ers; many singers, few clingers; lots of pastors, few wrestlers; many fears, few tears; much fashion, little passion; many interferers, few intercessors; many writers, but few fighters. Failing here, we fail everywhere."

That's hard to take because it's true. And that's why, when we come to a passage on prayer, we had better listen because here God has something to say to us that can change that decay in our lives and in our church.

The ninth chapter of the book of Daniel contains one of the greatest Old Testament prayers. In many respects, this illustration of prayer in the midst of prophecy is like an oasis in the middle of a desert. It is an example of what praying ought to be. Also in this chapter is the well-known prophecy of the seventy weeks. But the prophecy which gives this chapter its fame is two times shorter than the prayer which precedes it. I really believe we cannot understand the prophecy and its significance until we get into the prayer.

Life-Changing Prayer Is Motivated by the Word of God

When Daniel went into captivity with the rest of the Jews, he didn't have a copy of the Bible like we have today. There was obviously no New Testament, and vast portions of the Old Testament were not available. But when Daniel went into captivity, he did have some portions of the Old Testament. In particular, he had some of the writings of Jeremiah the prophet.

Jeremiah ministered in the time just previous to the captivity of the people of Judah. He was the last prophet to call out to those people to repent before the judgment of God fell upon them. Isaiah had prophesied many years earlier, and they wouldn't listen; but right up until the very last moment, Jeremiah cried out against the sin of Judah and called them to repentance. But they would not repent, and they were all carried away into captivity.

When Daniel was about 85 or 86, he was reading in Jeremiah; and I believe something jumped off the page into his heart that motivated his prayer in chapter 9. It must have been Jeremiah 25:8-11: "Therefore thus says the Lord of hosts: 'Because you have not heard My words, behold, I will send and take all the families of the north,' says the Lord, 'and Nebuchadnezzar the king of Babylon, My servant, and will bring them against this land, against its inhabitants, and against these nations all around, and will utterly destroy them, and make them an astonishment, a hissing, and perpetual desolations. Moreover I will take from them the voice of mirth and the voice of gladness, the voice of the bridegroom and the voice of the bride, the sound of the millstones and the light of the lamp. And this whole land shall be a desolation and an astonishment.'"

Daniel knew all about this. He had lived through almost seventy years of it. From the very beginning, Daniel had watched as the song had been taken out of the hearts of his people as they hung their harps on the willows and cried out for the day when they could go back to Jerusalem. He saw their captivity take the very life out of their Jewish culture and history. But that's not the part of the prophecy that caught Daniel's attention. It was the last part of verse 11 and following: "'And these nations shall serve the king of Babylon seventy years. Then it will come to pass, when seventy years are completed, that I will punish the king of Babylon and that nation, the land of the Chaldeans, for their iniquity,' says the Lord; 'and I will make it a perpetual desolation. So I will bring on that land all My words which I have pronounced against it, all that is written in this book, which Jeremiah has prophesied concerning all the nations. (For many nations and great kings shall be served by them also; and I will repay them according to their deeds and according to the works of their own hands.)'"

Daniel was in his early to mid-eighties at the time, depending on how old he was when he was taken captive. Now as he reads the prophecy of Jeremiah, he knows that almost seventy years have come to pass since he was carried away captive with the people. The prophecy gets hold of his heart because he begins to realize the time for the return of his people to Jerusalem is drawing near. He probably does not know whether the time is calculated from the first, second, or third deportation. But he does know the time is getting close. It's almost time for God to redeem His people

> "REPENTANCE IS NOT an emotion. It is not feeling sorry for your sins. It is a decision. It is deciding that you have been wrong in supposing that you could manage your own life and be your own god."
>
> EUGENE PETERSON

and take them back to their land. The prophecy got such a hold on Daniel's heart, he fell on his knees and began to pray.

Isn't it true that when we really come to grips with prophecy, it ought to have that kind of effect on us? Yet we so often get caught up in the exercise of understanding prophetic truth that we miss the whole point. The point of prophetic truth is that it ought to drive us to our knees even as it did Daniel. When Daniel read what God had to say, he couldn't stay the same. His prayer was motivated by the Word of God.

I think it is always proper before we open the Scripture to briefly ask for God's blessing and insight into the text. But if I understand the priority of the Word of God, prayer grows out of God's Word. When we read the Word of God and study it, as we come to grips with what it means, we find within us a prayer being formed that will take the Word of God and apply it to our very experience.

Life-Changing Prayer Is Measured by the Will of God

Daniel read in the book of Jeremiah that God was going to keep His people in captivity for seventy years, and then He was going to release them. A strange thing happens as he reads what God is going to do. He begins to pray that God will do what He's going to do. Basically he prays, "Lord, what You said You were going to do, that's what I want You to do."

If God has said He's going to do something, why should we pray? God knows His plan, and even when He reveals His plan to us, He expects us to pray over that plan. God revealed that His time was about up for the captive people. When Daniel got the truth about what God would do, he fell to his knees and began to pray in the will of God that God would do what He was going to do.

> **"The ninth chapter of Daniel is one of the most important chapters in the Bible. Spiritually it has one of the greatest Old Testament prayers; prophetically, it contains the most comprehensive outline of the End Times. The prayer is an example of what praying ought to be. It is a masterpiece for us to admire, a dramatic example of principles to follow."**
>
> Dr. David Jeremiah, *The Handwriting on the Wall–Secrets from the Prophecies of Daniel*

Sometimes I get the impression, even from my own prayers, that we have misunderstood the meaning of prayer. Prayer is not to get God to change His will. If you really believe that the will of God is perfect, then why would you want Him to change it? But we labor long at prayer trying to get God to change His will from what we think He is going to do, when our prayer really ought to be motivated out of our deep understanding of what the will of God is.

The will of God will never lead you contrary to the Word of God. When your prayer is motivated by the Word of God and you understand what God has said, then you can pray what God has already said to be His will. Prayer is not a device for getting our will done through heaven. It is a device for allowing God's will to be done on earth through us. That's why we are told to pray, "Thy kingdom come, Thy will be done" (Matthew 6:10, KJV). Prayer is not getting God to adjust His program to what we want. Prayer is adjusting our lives to the revealed will of God. When we pray, it isn't God who changes—it's us.

Life-Changing Prayer Is Manifested in Our Walk With God

Frequency of Prayer

There are two things about Daniel's life that come into focus when we examine his praying. First of all, there is his frequency of prayer. Prayer shouldn't just be something we do at a point in time. Prayer should be a part of our total life and being. For Daniel, prayer is the very fabric of his life.

Daniel 6:10 is a testimony to the frequency of Daniel's praying. When he knew there was a law against praying to anyone other than Darius, he went home and prayed to God "as was his custom since early days." When the crisis came, Daniel didn't change anything. He kept right on doing what he had always done. Maybe one of those prayers he prayed is this prayer in chapter 9.

Fervency of Prayer

Daniel's praying wasn't like ours so often is. He didn't see God as a divine servant to get him whatever he needed at a moment's notice. He didn't pop in front of God and say his thing and leave. Daniel was fervent in prayer.

What does it mean to be fervent in prayer? In the Old Testament culture there were certain things that accompanied fervent prayer.

The emotional involvement of a person who was praying fervently for the will of God to be done might include any of the following: The person might wear sackcloth (the garments of mourning), sit in an ash pile, put ashes on his head, or shave off the hair on his head. They may smite their breast, cry, tear their garments, fast, sigh, groan, sweat blood, agonize, pour out their heart, make oaths or sacrifices. Somehow our prayer lives don't seem to fit into that context. That's fervent praying.

Another element of fervent praying may involve fasting. Jesus fasted. Paul fasted. Early Church leaders fasted. In the Old Testament, Isaiah, Daniel, Esther, David, Hannah, Elijah, Ezra, Nehemiah, Zechariah, and others fasted. In Church history you learn that Martin Luther, John Calvin, John Knox, John and Charles Wesley, David Brainerd, George Mueller, and many more fasted. It's hard to find a great person of faith who didn't fast.

We are not commanded to fast in the New Testament. But that does not do away with the fact that sometimes fasting gets at this matter of fervency in our praying. It is a time in our lives when we say "No" to our physical wants and desires, and we prioritize the spiritual realm within us.

There are many times in the Bible when fasting occurs for a specific reason. In the Old Testament, people fasted because of private problems. For instance, Hannah fasted because she was barren. Sometimes in the Old Testament they fasted because of public disasters, sometimes because of personal grief. Sometimes in perplexity over a situation, sometimes because of a peril that was ahead.

Sometimes fasting took place in penitence over sin. Sometimes because of pity for friends. Sometimes in perplexity over the will of God. The New Testament teaches that certain demons could not be cast out except by prayer and fasting.

I haven't told you all this because I want you to start fasting. The point is that fasting is simply one measure indicating fervency in our relationship with God. I don't believe God is enamored with any emotionless, uninvolved relationship with Him.

Edgar Young Mullins gives an illustration to this point. A little monkey got loose from the organ grinder in the cold wintertime. He was freezing to death and sought warmth. He jumped on the sill of a house and looked through the window pane and saw a roaring fire. He found his way inside the room and sat there with his little paws raised to the fire but froze to death. The fire was only painted on a screen.

How many churches are like that? How many Christians are like that—fires painted on screens? With no emotion, no fervency, and no warmth? I wonder if we really believe what we say we believe if we're not willing to get involved. When we pray, we need to pray fervently. Read God's Word and see what God wants you to pray about. Then get involved frequently and fervently in talking to your God.

PERSONAL QUESTIONS

1. Read Daniel 9:1-4.

   a. How do we know prayer was a regular, important part of Daniel's life? (See Daniel 6.)

   b. What in verses 1-2 motivated Daniel to pray?

   c. Have you been motivated to pray after spending time in God's Word? If so, how would you describe the content of your prayer?

d. What actions did Daniel take while he was praying?

e. How did Daniel begin his prayer?

f. How did Daniel describe God in his prayer?

g. What are some attributes of God that you can praise Him for today?

2. Explain the relationship between prayer and God's Word.

   a. How does understanding this relationship impact your prayer life?

   b. What steps can you take in your own life to deepen the connection between reading God's Word and praying?

GROUP QUESTIONS

1. Turn to Daniel 9:1-4 together.

   a. When did Jeremiah minister to the people of Judah?

   b. What did Daniel realize as he was reading from Jeremiah? (verse 2)

   c. What accompanied fervent prayer during the Old Testament? (verse 3)

2. Discuss the connection between prayer and God's will.

   a. Knowing what God was going to do, how did Daniel pray?

   b. How should we pray when God reveals His plan to us? And how should we pray when God doesn't reveal His plan to us?

3. Discuss the spiritual practice of fasting.

a. Who are some examples of people who fasted in the Old Testament? In the New Testament?

b. What are some reasons given for why people fasted?

c. Have you ever fasted for a specific reason? If so, share how fasting helped you be more fervent in prayer.

DID YOU KNOW?

There was a requirement in the Law given through Moses that the Israelite land was to lie fallow every seventh year—a Sabbath of rest for the land just as there was a weekly Sabbath rest for man (Leviticus 25:4). But Israel failed to give the land its Sabbath rest for hundreds of years (Leviticus 26:43). That was one of the reasons God removed Israel from the land into captivity in Babylon for seventy years—one year for each seven-year cycle they had failed to observe. Jeremiah understood this and told Israel how long her captivity would be: seventy years (Jeremiah 25:11).

ADDITIONAL RESOURCES
by Dr. David Jeremiah

The Handwriting on the Wall

From being a young captive to becoming the king's wisest advisor, the life of Daniel is a study of faithfulness and courage in a foreign land amidst difficult circumstances. With three correlating study guides, this book uncovers much of the prophecy discussed in the book of Daniel and studies the life of a godly man who always remained true to his identity in the Lord. Understanding prophecy opens the pathway to dynamic living in our life today and studying the book of Daniel can encourage us to live in faith today and anticipate the future with confidence.

Agents of the Apocalypse

What is the Apocalypse? What events will surround the Apocalypse? Who will take center stage at that time? In this book, Dr. David Jeremiah details the ten most prominent players in the book of Revelation—those who are the primary agents of the Apocalypse. Through this study, learn about the key characters and events in the End Times and strengthen your vocation in the Lord. Through the book of Revelation, be encouraged to stand firm in the face of worsening circumstances.

People Are Asking … Is This the End?

We live in difficult times—it seems our nation is more divided than ever before, and our world seems more fractured each day. While reading the headlines many may be asking, "Is this the end?" As we navigate through the issues that plague our times, we mustn't lose heart and need to turn to God for answers to our questions. In this book, Dr. David Jeremiah delves into the signs of the times, examining the prophetic clues in Scripture that help us understand the world around us—and helps us establish a clear path forward.

Agents of Babylon

The kingdom of Babylon is notorious for its cruelty and immorality. It is often seen as a symbol of the world's worst evil. Sadly, there are many parallels between this kingdom, described in the book of Daniel, and the world today. In this book, Dr. David Jeremiah studies the prophetic markers and visions mentioned in the book of Daniel and carefully examines the most prominent players in it—characters Dr. Jeremiah calls "the agents of Babylon." This study offers insight to their significance and gives practical life application from the book of Daniel and hope for the future.

Each of these resources was created from a teaching series by Dr. David Jeremiah. Contact Turning Point for more information about correlating materials.

For pricing information and ordering, contact us at

P.O. Box 3838
San Diego, CA 92163
(800) 947-1993
www.DavidJeremiah.org

STAY CONNECTED

to Dr. David Jeremiah

Take advantage of two great ways to let Dr. David Jeremiah give you spiritual direction every day!

Turning Points Magazine and Devotional

Receive Dr. David Jeremiah's magazine, *Turning Points*, each month:

- Thematic study focus
- 48 pages of life-changing reading
- Relevant articles
- Special features
- Daily devotional readings
- Bible study resource offers
- Live event schedule
- Radio & television information

Request *Turning Points* magazine today!

(800) 947-1993
www.DavidJeremiah.org/Magazine

Daily Turning Point E-Devotional

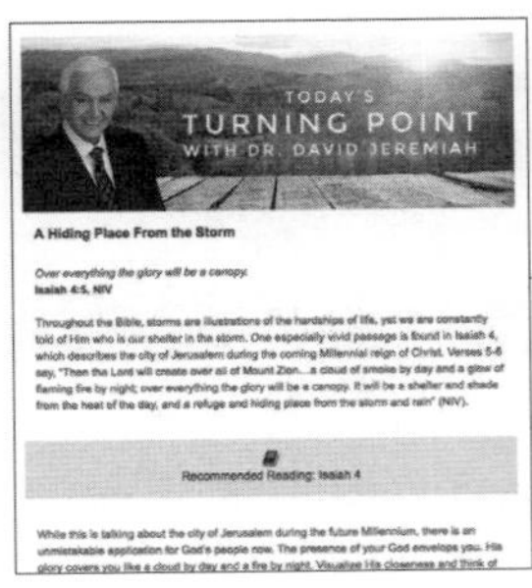

TODAY'S
TURNING POINT
WITH DR. DAVID JEREMIAH

A Hiding Place From the Storm

Over everything the glory will be a canopy.
Isaiah 4:5, NIV

Throughout the Bible, storms are illustrations of the hardships of life, yet we are constantly told of Him who is our shelter in the storm. One especially vivid passage is found in Isaiah 4, which describes the city of Jerusalem during the coming Millennial reign of Christ. Verses 5-6 say, "Then the Lord will create over all of Mount Zion...a cloud of smoke by day and a glow of flaming fire by night; over everything the glory will be a canopy. It will be a shelter and shade from the heat of the day, and a refuge and hiding place from the storm and rain" (NIV).

Recommended Reading: Isaiah 4

While this is talking about the city of Jerusalem during the future Millennium, there is an unmistakable application for God's people now. The presence of your God envelops you. His glory covers you like a cloud by day and a fire by night. Visualize His closeness and think of

Start your day off right! Find words of inspiration and spiritual motivation waiting for you on your computer every morning! Receive a daily e-devotion communication from David Jeremiah that will strengthen your walk with God and encourage you to live the authentic Christian life.

Request your free e-devotional today!

(800) 947-1993
www.DavidJeremiah.org/Devo